# Death by Lobster:
# Living with Allergies

## By Ben Cober

# Table of Contents

# Introduction

Let's just go ahead and lay it all out here:

- Anacardium occidentale (Cashew)
- Arachis hypogaea (Peanuts)
- Aspergillus Niger (Fungus that causes black mold)
- Bertholletia excels (Brazil nut)
- Brachyura (Crabs)
- Canis lupus familiaris (Dogs)
- Caridea (Shrimp)
- Castanea (Chestnut)
- Corylus avallana (Hazelnut)
- Dermatophagoides pteronyssinus (Dust mites)
- Eggs
- Feathers
- Felis catus (Cats)
- Poaceae spp. (Grass)
- Nephropidae (Lobster)
- Periplaneta Americana and Blatella germanica (American and German cockroach)
- Pinaceae (Pine nuts)
- Pistacia vera (Pistachio)
- Prunus dulcis (Almonds)
- Ragweed
- Trees
- Weeds

**And previously chocolate, penicillin, and insect stings

That right there is the comprehensive list of everything that can temporarily or permanently incapacitate me, bringing me to my knees or to my grave. They're my various types of Kryptonite, my exposed heel, just waiting for an arrow. That exhaustive list is what I'm allergic to.

I can hear you scoffing already. Most likely, your exposure to allergies is probably a kid you remember from elementary school with a pocket full of tissues and a bright red, runny nose who was always sucking snot in class. She was gross. Maybe it was more severe: maybe she was quarantined to a special part of the cafeteria during lunch because she was allergic to something in that day's mystery meat. It made her "weird," "foreign," or "outcast." Maybe you were on a flight in 2014 that had to be diverted because someone on board opened their peanuts, and there was a child on board allergic to their air-born dust particles, and you rolled your eyes and went "really?!"

But allergies aren't just here to stay, they're growing in prevalence. Now I'm not typically a self-diagnosing sneezer scrolling through the pages of WebMD; however, they do have a pretty interesting list of cited statistics about allergies in America today:

- 20%: Percentage of Americans who have either allergy or asthma symptoms
- 55%: Percentage of Americans who test positive to one or more allergens
- 8%: Percentage of Americans who have asthma
- $7.9 billion: Estimated annual cost of allergies to the US healthcare system and businesses
- Four million: Number of US work days lost each year due to hay fever (see boss, it's a legit reason to call in sick!)
- 30,000: Number of ER visits in America each year due to food allergies
- 15%: Percentage of Americans who believe they have a food allergy
- 4%: Percentage of Americans who actually have a food allergy
- 3,447: Number of deaths from asthma in America in 2007

- 20: A rough estimate of how many children in the US die annually from food allergies (Bock SA, Munoz-Furlong A, Sampson HA. J Allergy Clin Immunol 2001; 107:191)

Daily life with allergies isn't just all sniffles and Allegra though. I can't count how many times in school my eyes were so blurry with allergy-induced tears that I couldn't read my tests. Or there was that time clutching my chest straining to breathe, feeling like I was drowning, after my first hayride around a pumpkin patch. And there were numerous ambulance rides to the ER, where my gathered family was starting to put their words together about how to say goodbye (sounds a little dramatic, but entirely true).

But that's not what this book is about. It's not a sob story (actually, many of these incidents related in these pages are kind of funny looking back on them now), and I never felt like an outcast or that I was ostracized. This book isn't going to be "The Top Ten Ways to Protect Your Child from the World of Their Allergies and Ensure They Grow Up Terrified, Anti-Social, Paranoid, and Risk-Averse." And it's not going to be a scientific, peer-reviewed journal on the cause, treatment, and cure (or extreme lack-there-of) of allergies. I'm not a doctor, and neither are you (probably, or else you'd be reading something else).

No, I'm someone who for 31 years (and let's be fair, probably only 26 "aware" years) has lived with a menu of various allergies that can take one of those exhaustive, classic diner menus and turn it into three, edible dishes. Yes, precautions were taken throughout; and yes, I've developed various neuroticisms that I don't even notice any more for the sake of self-preservation. For instance, when I read a restaurant menu, I begin by eliminating everything I know I'm allergic to; or the fact that when I visit a friend's house which is also home to a cat, I can't sit down on any fabric (and I'm eager to suggest anything, ANYTHING, to get us to go somewhere else).

What this book is about is proof of life. Proof that you (or your kid(s)) can live a fun, exciting, great, risk-taking life without being imprisoned in a bubble and the endless *woosh* * woosh* of their helicopter parents hovering above. Sure, there are some simple rules to keep you alive; and yes, when the ragweed or pollen count sky-rockets, sometimes there's no amount of Benadryl that can keep you well (or awake), so it's a day you call in sick and curl up on the couch with Netflix and three boxes of tissues.

However, I've lived a full life thus far in spite of allergies and asthma: I've climbed more than six miles above 12,000 feet; I've SCUBA-dove deeper than 60' for 45 minutes; gotten lifeguard certified; I've spent the summer outdoors learning from and teaching at summer camps; I've run through fields, hiked through jungles, and explored dusty ruins across the world; raced sailboats, played soccer, and even completed a marathon.

There is a wonderful, deep, beautiful world out there, filled with delightful people, tasty dishes, and jaw-dropping scenery, as well as ragweed, pollens, and molds; and I'm here to tell you that you can, and should, go live every experience you can.

# Chapter 1: Egg Beaters

In my experience, there are four ways to determine if you have an allergy:

1. A formal skin test; which let me tell you, is the absolute bee's knees. I'll go into depth on this bad boy in a minute.
2. A formal eating test, which is excitingly terrifying. More on this in a moment.
3. Touch something, then break out in a violently itchy rash that elevates off your skin with hives; which, adequately named, look like something's hatching under your skin and getting ready to pop out.
4. Eat something, and experience a reaction anywhere between an itchy throat, kind of like you haven't had a drink of water in a few hours, to waking up in an emergency room as someone pulls you away from a bright light.

Eggs. Eggs is a bit of a blurry memory, mostly formed out of what I've been told as an account from my parents. (My memory of things prior to three years old is a bit hazy.) I don't think I'm blocking anything out... I hope I'm not blocking anything out....no, I'm sure everything was fine. At any rate, the story goes that I was hanging out by the kitchen counter in my dashingly fashionable diapers, chillin' with my mother while she made a pie. In some families, ice cream is the thing; in others, its cake; while others worship the almighty adorable possibilities of cupcakes. In my family, it's pie. In all its glorious iterations, pie is featured prominently at all of our family gatherings, and apparently has been for generations. If pie is the royal family of my lineage's dessert delights, apple and pumpkin are king and queen.

Hanging out, the curious little bundle of chubby pink and electrified blond hair that I was, I smoothly reached up and snatched some raw pie dough from the thin lake my mother had just finished rolling out, and jammed it into my mouth like all tiny tots do: knuckles first, dripping with spit. I have no memory of the taste; but I assure you, the love of pie is genetic (I guess technically stopping with me now), so it was in my blood to delight in the sweetness of the sugar and flour, and the tangy, saltiness of the butter is probably one of the sources of my love of 'salt over sweet' to this very day.

And then things went full bummer. Babies cry, I get that; in fact, in my adult life, I've found I'm highly sensitive to it, often considering parachuting out of commercial jets as parents make the decision to torture their babies whose ear canals haven't developed the strength to equalize ascending and descending cabin pressure. But I wailed and howled with the best of them, and my stomach began to try and eject this horrible, foreign substance. But not in the kind of cute, kind of funny way that little fat babies throw up a little on their chin or their bib, and look up at you with their glistening, doughy eyes as if to say "I'm so sorry, I made that, please don't be mad." It was a bit more like Linda Blair in The Exorcist after eating a bit too much pea soup.

After a trip to the emergency room that evening, alive and still astoundingly adorable, I was ok. But the doctors informed my parents that I was allergic to eggs; and where there's smoke, there's fire. If a kid has one food allergy, there's likely to be more. I can't say for sure, but I could safely guess that that evening was the beginning of my mother's high blood pressure.

It's worth noting too that, on a not too dissimilar evening, not too far off from the aforementioned, my brother, 12 years my senior, was heating up the stove to cook popcorn while babysitting me one night. As he was working throughout the kitchen, most likely dancing with himself to Foreigner, I waddled over and reached high up to the stove (potentially having drug a chair across the floor for extra height), placing my hand right on the red-hot stove coils. Kind of like in that scene in Home Alone where Joe Pesci grabs the doorknob from which McCauley Caulkin hangs an iron.

Thanks bro.

# Chapter 2: Ida May's Kitchen

These early years were tough: we were still figuring out the things which might cause bad allergic reactions. But it gets easier, I promise. If a lifetime of learning about allergies could be made into an event, I'd liken it to downhill skiing... on a double black diamond... without poles... before anyone taught you anything. It's absolutely crazy in the beginning, flying down so fast that the world's a blur. You're smashing into moguls, yard-sale-ing all over the place, and people are screaming at you all the time. People on the lifts are pointing down at you, some are laughing and egging (ha ha) you on, some are genuinely concerned, but you're moving too fast with a mouth full of snow to yell "I'm new at this!" But as you rocket your way down, someone throws you a pair of poles (maybe your allergist), you start learning to dodge a mogul here and there; and by the time you make it to the bottom, all you have to do is glide along and watch out for the other skiers sliding in and out of the crowd. (That's unlisted ingredients you're allergic to on restaurant menus). And, you've got a great story to tell in front of the big sky-lodge fireplace!

In the good ol' days, my family's summer vacation was always to Myrtle Beach. Throughout the '80s and early '90s, my parents and brother would load up into the family station wagon and drive down from Connecticut to the neon and putt-putt golf-saturated beaches of South Carolina. At the same time, grandparents, great aunts and uncles, and cousins would saddle up in Pennsylvania and meet us there. The blur of warm nostalgia is mixing with actual memory, but I can remember the turnaround of the two-towered, light pink hotel that the whole family always stayed in. I know it had a pool, and there are fuzzy memories of playing catch with my brother with a rubber lion while I wore confidence-boosting arm floaties.

Much of our time involved the "elders" pulling their beach chairs just close enough to the ocean for the surf to barely wash over their feet, big floppy sun hats and books in tow, and chatting away the day, while my brother and I ran through the surf. For me, evenings were filled with trying out various putt-putt establishments along the main stretch, the Moby Dick-themed one burning the deepest memory in my brain. I mean come on, you walked through a whale! The fondest memory though was going to my grandparents' hotel room, where my grandmother, Ida May, would fix lunch.

Their little kitchenette had a counter with stools, and my grandfather Pap and I would saddle up in them, usually still in wet swim trunks from the beach and kicking off sand onto the tiles, and would chatter like we were at a diner, teasing my grandmother about the service. He'd talk about the long wait times and mixing up orders, and I'd always be clarifying the need to have the crust trimmed off my bread. She'd tease us right back, not taking any crap from the mouthy clientele. Pap would laugh until he wheezed. He called it "Ida May's Kitchen."

My family likes shellfish. It can't be our ancestors; the Black Forest is pretty well landlocked in Germany and is more than 300 miles to the nearest body of saltwater. Stateside, my family's roots are deep in rural Pennsylvania; and contrary to popular belief, cultivating fields of gently-waving lobsters was not as popular an agricultural pursuit as you've been led to believe.

So it's got to be Connecticut, where my parents moved after my dad finished graduate school in the late '70s, and where I was born. Yes, I was born in the heart of a rich tradition of lobstering and whaling, although I've never been tested for whale allergies. Lobster though; man, it's ironic.

The thing is: I love shellfish, too! Note that I said "shellfish," not "seafood." They were a blast to play with as a kid. Every open chance I had as a kid, and even later when I went back to visit, my mother would take me to Chaffinch Island, where I'd dash between tide pools for hours with my little bucket collecting snails, crabs, and hermit crabs. There's photographic evidence of me playing on the kitchen floor (after I was banned from standing on chairs to reach the kitchen counter) with live lobsters, their claws still bound with bright blue or red rubber bands from the grocery store.

Heck, my cousin Mike, who is that legendary kind of relative every kid dreams of having, was an undercover cop in Baltimore (and today enjoys a cushy desk job in the same precinct). He had a buddy who was a crabber in the Charm City; and each summer, Mike would bring two huge bags of fresh, live blue crabs to the homestead in Pennsylvania. Everyone would gather for the feast with claw crackers, mallets, and bibs at the ready, and I'd play around with the crabs in the backyard grass until they were ushered into the kitchen where they faced a fate I couldn't yet comprehend. Sadly, by the time this tradition started though, I wasn't allowed to sit at the long picnic table covered in a red/white checkerboard tablecloth, where my aunts and uncles gabbed while butter and shell flew. No, I sat at a card table, by myself, about 20 feet away, with a hotdog. Because we learned: Shellfish were the bomb; seafood was not.

On one fateful evening in Myrtle Beach, after a joyous day of toes in the Atlantic and chasing neon green golf balls off the putt-putt Astroturf that had been struck too hard, the family headed out for dinner. All I remember is lobster traps; that was the theme: lots and lots of lobster traps. We shuffled in to various wooden booths overlooking the ocean near sunset, and I scootched my little toosh onto the long plank of wood, sliding on my Osh-Kosh-B-Gosh jean shorts and navy blue polo over beside my mom.

Dinner was not particularly memorable, in my mind at least. But when we got up to leave, that's when the banshee scream came from my mother. From the edge of my shorts to my knees, the back of my thighs were covered in bright red, swollen lumps. It looked like I had sat in a fire ant nest. This was our first exposure to hives.

You see, shellfish is a finger food, that's what makes it so darn appealing to a little kid. Our parents are always telling us to use your fork and knife. Don't use your fingers. Don't play with your food. But with shellfish, you get these weapons of focused destruction! The claw crackers, the Medieval mallet with spikes, the itty bitty fork, a bib for the massive amounts of butter running down, and a bucket of the golden stuff sitting next to your plate. Then all the while you're grabbing these limbs and cracking them apart with this arsenal and your bare hands, a Jacques Cousteau Brawler, and slurping down the sweet meat.

But, there comes a point when you have done all the damage you can possibly do, and you have to get up from the table and move on. So when you're sitting on a bench, what do you do? You put your hands down, and push your body up from your seat to leave.

So for almost two hours, I had been sitting in the greasy, buttery, shell-fishy residue of a hundred hands that had slid across that bench that day. And as I stood up to leave, the backs of my legs had become massive, pink, pulsing welts covered in hives – accompanied by the delightful soundtrack of my mother's screams.

I'm fortunate: skin contact doesn't lead to internal illness, just a lot of itching and soreness. It's a strange thing we discovered when we got back home: before they're cooked, me and shellfish like shrimp, lobster, crab, clams, mussels, and more can be best buddies, dead or alive. But the minute they get cooked, something gets released from inside them and they become a ticking time bomb of near-death experiences if they approach my skin.

Whatever, I was partial to Ida May's ham sandwiches anyway.

# Chapter 3: The Best Science Has to Offer!?

What if, to determine if your body would get sick from cancer, the doctor gave you an injection of cancerous cells? What if to figure out if your immune system wouldn't be too psyched to get AIDS, your trusted physician injected you with a small dose of HIV, and just watched what happened?

That is exactly the state of the allergy-testing environment today, and has been at least for the last 26 years. True, I've learned that as recently as 2014, you can send off blood to places like the Mayo Clinic to have it evaluated for the more serious allergies; but prior to that, all I knew was what I'm about to describe to you.

After these little egg and shellfish incidents, it was time to get tested to figure out what else might be lying dormant in my system. The results, to say the least, were way less awesome than locating a high concentration of midi-chlorians or a latent X-Mutant gene.

You'd think, in this kind of test, maybe they'd draw a little bit of blood, send it off to a lab, they'd run it through some state-of-the-technological art machine, and a computer would spit out all the things that should not mix with this blood, from Arachis hypogaea to anthrax. But nope; it's a "poke it and see what happens" kind of science.

So every few years I have to go into my allergist's office to do one of these painstaking, expensive tests, because here's the hilarious thing about allergies: they come and go. Some, like shellfish and peanuts, your allergist will tell you that you'll pretty much have for life. Others though, like various pollen strains – or heck, PENICILLIN – can gain and lose favor with your immune system like a flip-flopping brother on Game of Thrones. So you have to regularly go in to find out who the good guys are, and who the bad guys are.

For those of you who haven't yet experienced this medical delight, let me break it down for you. You arrive at your allergist after being advised to "clear your schedule after the appointment." The nurse instructs you to take your shirt off, "I'll be back in a moment." Somewhere between 10 minutes and six hours (exaggerating a wee bit), she returns to find you shivering in the meat-locker that is your examination room (because whoever's watching the security camera finds it hilarious to watch you shiver as you read every allergy-related poster in the room 15 times, trying to convince yourself that they're interesting). In her hand is a tray; and on that tray is a huge array of needles, like she's leaving some kind of sterile heroin den, and a rack of tiny vials, maybe up to around 40, all labelled in itty bitty indecipherable text.

And the fun begins.

One by careful one, the nurse pricks your back with a needle that contains a tiny drop of SOME sort of allergen: maybe you're allergic to it, maybe you're not. But her tray contains all the most common ones. Then she grabs a little blue pen and numbers the prick she made on your back. Before the ink dries, she's made another prick above it with a different allergen, and is labelling it. This continues until she's made an entire arch up and down your back, like some sort of tortuous half-McDonald's sign.

But we're not done there friend, OH-ho no we're not. Now you lay your arms on your thighs, palms up, and she does the same thing to that soft, tender part of your forearms. Two rows of pricks on both forearms, all numbered. They've got to be thorough; they've got to test it all.

Squeamish yet? Strap in, sister. Because then she leaves, giving you one final rule that you must endure for the next 15-30 minutes:

"Remember, don't itch anything!"

As you cock your head in disbelief and the door closes behind her, your body begins to swell, kind of like that scene in Gremlins when the evil Gremlins get wet. All the various little pricks begin to itch, on your lower back, your delts, on your spine at the base of your neck, and up and down your forearm. Your skin grows hot as they grow larger and bigger, and you can't. Touch. Anything. All you want to do, ALL you want to do, is fall into a sandpaper factory and roll around. But you can't. There are many rules unclarified: you're never told not to blare some Journey; you're never told not to pull all the paper off the roll on the bench and build a fleet of paper airplanes; heck, you could order pizza to the room. But there is one rule you cannot break:

Do. Not. Scratch.

When the time is up and you've reached your breaking point, the little nurse bounds back in, cheerful and happy like she just got back from a first date. "Ok, how're we doing?" is the typical question. Murder is inappropriate, I always need to remind myself.

She then takes a pair of calipers and measures how wide each hive/welt is (think of measuring the width of the base of a pink, evil mountain) and how high the welt rose off your skin (the height of the mountain), and records all of these. From some testing records I got from my allergist, these are referred to the "wheel" and "flare," respectively. Any wheels that exceed a diameter of two (I'm going to assume that's centimeters, not feet, but my chart doesn't specify) means you test positive, and that's now on your allergy laundry list.

Once this whole procedure is done, which honestly memory serves me is around two hours, you're given plenty of anti-itch cream (cortisone), and sent on your merry way, with results to come shortly. Skin is itching and achy, and you feel like you've been through war.

And that's what I do every few years. Every single time, I'm hopeful for negative results for peanuts, eggs, or shellfish, dreaming of PB&J sandwiches, omelets, and crawfish boils. And every time I come out finding that there's some kind of grass pollen in the South I no longer have to worry about, but now both German and American cockroaches are to be avoided.

WHAT!?

Science!

# Chapter 4: Eat It or/and Die!

But the science gets better.

Let me tee this up for you.

In the first decade of my adorable life, I was allergic to four foods:

1.  Eggs
2.  Nuts
3.  Shellfish
4.  Chocolate

I was born on October 11. Do you realize what affect those allergies have on one of the greatest holidays known to mankind, also made wonderful for being just two weeks after my birthday?!

Here's how Halloween went down. I would be something awesome. Childhood highlights include a tap-dancing spider, a little old man, and a fully-operational Star Destroyer made out of a refrigerator box.

"Back in my day," aka the early '90s, you were entirely safe to run around the neighborhood at night, in the dark, without reflective clothing, without your parents. I also lived in a simple, three-street subdivision where every road ended in a cul-de-sac except one.

I'd rampage throughout the 89-home neighborhood with three or four buddies, filling up pillow-cases (usually puffy-painted by my mother) with an unimaginable bounty of candy, long before the guilt-filled, chastising days of uncool sugar-free, gluten-free, fat-free, awesome-free candy.

If we were lucky enough for Halloween to be on a Friday or Saturday night, we headed to one of our basements for one of the best traditions of childhood: a sleepover. There we would dump out our candy hoards and count through them, like the dragon Smaug swimming through his gold coins, pouring over the value of our booty. I, unlike the others, had a very methodical approach to this ritual:

1. Remove all chocolate from my stash, and put it to the side. This means any mini candy bars, like Hershey's, CRUNCH, 3 Musketeers, little Kisses, or Tootsie Rolls. (heck, even the Blow-pops have chocolate on the inside)
2. Remove anything that has a nut in it, like Almond Joy, actual little bags of nuts, Reese's, Brittle, etc.

But the shenanigans did not stop there, folks. THEN you've got to read the labels of everything with a label (if you're fortunate enough), to find those two alarming words: "MAY CONTAIN"; or, a little more understandably, "PROCESSED IN A FACILITY THAT PROCESSES EGGS, NUTS, CHOCOLATE, etc…"

**Now for some ART: Angry Rant Tangent.** Really, "may contain"?! Do you realize how ridiculous those two words sound to someone with a food allergy? How do you not know what is being made in your factory!? How do you not know what food is on what conveyor belt?! If I invite you over for dinner, does my invitation say "House may contain a rabid lion" or "House may contain polio"?! No, I KNOW what's in my own home! When you buy an iPhone, does the box say "may contain waffles, a goat, and between three and seven oranges"? NO, it most certainly does not! This is your business, potentially the lifeblood of thousands of workers you employ. If you don't know, FIGURE IT OUT. Don't guess what's going on in your factories; be certain!

Ok, thanks for enduring that rant, back to the story. So there's even a fourth step, once the chocolate, nuts, and ingredient lists have been removed. The "guesses." The guesses are what you can't quite be sure about. It's in a wrapper, but there's no label or ingredients. MIGHT have chocolate, there COULD be a nut in the middle of that green candy… These usually took the form of the foil-wrapped candies you see commonly around Easter, like little foil eggs, and the kind of individually-wrapped candy your grandmother might've kept in a dish on the piano.

Then my friends would swoop in like hyenas and take all my allergy food. (Anything the vultures didn't confiscate, my parents were happy to requisition when I got home) "Why not trade!?" you exclaim, (you brilliant opportunist, you!) But my friends were smart, they knew my allergy candy had no value for me – I couldn't eat it, so why trade me anything valuable for it?

So what are you left with after you apportion all of your hard-earned, but useless (to you) candy out to your fellow ghouls and goblins?

1. Twizzlers
2. Skittles
3. Smarties
4. %$#$ %^@%ing Candy Corn

This is the core reason today why the only candies I really like are Twizzlers and Skittles, and generally despise Smarties and Candy Corn.

So this was the pattern up until the age of ten, when a single trip to the allergist changed everything.

Ok, one thing.

I had recently endured one of these delightful adventures in "stabbing your back and seeing what happens," which is inversely difficult to sit still and not itch the younger you are. The results came back a little later; and weirdly enough, chocolate and eggs didn't register very high on the allergy-o-meter.

So the allergist wanted me to come in for a "challenge." A challenge means that your skin test scored so low, but you used to be very allergic to this thing, so there's a small chance that you might not be allergic to it any more.
So you have to eat it.

That's right folks; if you thought the skin test was archaic, the eating test means you eat the thing you've been told by everyone to avoid like the plague for your entire life, and you've developed habits and routines to watch out for it and steer clear of it, and now they're going to make you eat it.

And watch what happens.

Science!

So the big day arrives, and my mom drives me to the grocery store to pick up one, single, original HERSHEY'S milk chocolate bar. Yes, just the plain old one in the silver foil, brown wrapping, and bold black lettering. To me, she's holding a bar of anthrax mixed with meth. She's holding death row.

We drive the 20 minutes to the allergist, the little monster sliding around in the back seat in its plastic bag, threatening to leap into the front seat, unwrap itself, jump into my mouth, and kill me. I am being led to my execution.

At the allergist, we're led into a room, but a room like I had never seen before. As I remember, it was stark white. On the walls, instead of the normal "here's what pollen looks like under a microscope" and "here's what an inflamed lung looks like" posters, the walls were covered in serious life-saving equipment. I very clearly remember seeing an AED machine (electric paddles if your heart stops) and an oxygen tank with a mask. They explained that they had plenty of epinephrine on hand, in case I went in to anaphylactic shock. (As I explain to friends from time to time, epinephrine does not save your life. It only delays the reaction until you can make it to the ER for more effective treatment).

The allergist is there as we open the brown death, and she begins to break apart the little chocolate bricks that make up a full bar of HERSHEY'S milk chocolate. When she's done, and after much reassuring, she tells me to eat one of the little blocks.

Eat chocolate?!

My eyes darted to my mother's, then to the allergist's, back to the chocolate; continuously making this triangle of visual doubt. My mother looked terrified. The allergist calmly reassured me. I took a deep breath, closed my eyes, and popped the little morsel into my mouth.

I had never tasted chocolate before. (We had originally discovered this one through the skin prick test). It began to melt a bit in between my teeth, drizzling down between my gums and my cheeks. It was softer than I had expected, but still had a bit of a *crack* sound as it broke down, and got squishier as the pieces gently gave way and got smaller. I encountered weird flavors that were new to me: a sweet, foreign version of sugar, teasing the back of my tongue; and a strange, bitter after-taste that hung on the tip of my tongue and on the back of my throat. It was everywhere: the poison left black spots between my teeth, worked deep under my tongue and between my cheeks, and down the back of my throat and into my stomach where I could not get it out. My heart raced.

The allergist waited in the room to watch me swallow it, making sure I didn't' spit it out. Then cheerfully said, "I'll be back in 15 minutes!" and briskly walked out. I had a million questions about my fate, future, and the current biological reactions happening in my body – but she had other things to attend to. I stared at my mom, wide-eyed, and she stared right back at me, tightly clutching her purse. I don't think either of us blinked once within the full 15 minutes, the second hand ticking by on big white clock above us.

And I waited. I waited to feel my chest tighten and my esophagus slowly begin to close. I waited to start gasping like a fish out of water while my eyes swelled shut, my vision becoming a pinhole until it disappeared. I waited for the stomach turning sickness that felt like a huge octopus stretching and pushing to escape my stomach.
But it never came. Not even the faint tickle in the back of my throat. I was all right.

The doctor returned. "So, how're we doin'?" Cheerful as can be.

"I – I don't feel anything. I feel fine!" I said, my mother looking on with quiet dread.

"Great," the doctor responded. "Let's double the dose!"

What?! And thus unfolded why this was a two-hour ordeal. Every 15 minutes, as long as I didn't have a reaction, we doubled the amount of chocolate I ate. So after I survived the first mini brick, I ate two mini bricks. Then four mini bricks. And so on until I had eaten the entire chocolate bar.

What kind of logic is that?! "Well, the first bullet didn't kill him. Shoot him twice."

"He's still alive, sergeant!"

"Well then shoot him four times!"

It just blew me away as a kid, and still does today. Once again, this thing I'd been told to avoid with every ounce of my being for years, I was then being told to eat it…more of it…until I got sick.

But I never did. I never got sick. I was ok. At some point between ages three and seven, I outgrew my chocolate allergy. And that's another disconcerting thing about living with food allergies, and how they can come and go from your immune system. Let's say you're allergic to…blueberries. For years, your friends and family might be accommodating you, preparing meals without blueberries or choosing not to order family-style dishes with blueberries. For years you've been making excuses, "oh sorry, none for me, I'm allergic to blueberries." Only to find out one day that you've been inadvertently lying, for years.

Think about the implications if you were allergic to latex...
Anyway, back to childhood innocence. On the drive home
from the allergist, Mom and I swung into the grocery store,
and I picked out my first packet of Oreos and my very first,
ice-cold, half-gallon of chocolate milk. At home, I sat at our
kitchen counter and consumed them both, twisting the Oreos
and dunking them into the sweet brown milk, just like I had
seen on TV and my friends had done for years in the school
cafeteria.

Victory never tasted so sweet!

One month later I returned to the allergist to challenge the
egg allergy. My mom had nervously spent the morning
making scrambled eggs, the strange and foreign smell sizzling
throughout the kitchen.

I began by eating a single thimbleful of freshly scrambled
eggs.

And finished six minutes later vomiting into a garbage can
and having to call in sick to school two days in a row while
my insides heaved into a bucket next to the couch.

Thanks immune system. Fist bump.

# Chapter 5: Trouble in Paradise

When you live with food allergies, there's immense safety in familiarity. Frequenting the same restaurants in your hometown and always ordering the same thing, or only eating home-cooked meals, goes a long way in ensuring that you never eat anything you're allergic to.

But where's the fun in that?

I grew up in a family that strongly encouraged travel, both domestically and internationally. I was sincerely fortunate that, by the time I had graduated high school, I had travelled throughout Great Britain, Germany, Austria, Switzerland, Italy (speaking Latin, poorly), the Caribbean, Israel, a few excursions to Canada, and more than half the states the U.S. has to offer. (I grew up in Cincinnati, OH). I will never, ever, ever be able to put a value on these experiences, and what they have done for me, and my to-be-conceived children, in terms of confidence-building, resourcefulness, knowledge, and a far greater appreciation for the human condition than I otherwise would've had.

But that doesn't mean I almost didn't die doing it.

You see, when you travel to another country (heck, even another part of your own country), there are wildly different approaches to how food is described in menus, and how wait-staff interpret your questions. This problem can be compounded by how much the wait-staff actually care about or believe your food allergy, and even more if there's a language barrier. "Is this fried in peanut oil?" or "do you fry your French fries in the same basket as you do your shrimp?" can both be met with eye rolls or halfhearted investigation.

At the same time, ingredients might crop up in your dish that weren't listed on the menu. Case in point: just this week, I was out to one of my city's best Thai restaurants (I love Thai), and after carefully scanning the menu (we'll get to those techniques later), I chose a noodle dish that listed out all the ingredients in detail: glass noodles, green and red peppers, onions, mushrooms, and chicken. When the dish arrived, it was literally and very obviously (wish it could always be that easy) covered in peanuts. I said, "I'm so sorry, the menu didn't list peanuts, I'm very allergic. Could I please get a version made without?" and the waitress was apologetic and happy to accommodate.

But it's not always that easy to spot the allergy infestation. Sometimes it lies in secret, waiting, hiding behind something that looks delicious and enticing...

After the Myrtle Beach years, my family developed an obsession for the island of St. John in the US Virgin Islands. For the uninitiated, St. John is the little, under-developed brother of nearby St. Thomas; a bustling metropolis by Caribbean standards. St. John is dotted with quiet, small, beautiful beaches, and high-rising mountains covered with thick jungle in between. For tourists, a variety of stunning villas are nestled among the palms all around the rim of the island, rented out for weeks at a time by their owners. And all across the island are upscale (at least by price) restaurants in which they can dine.

The island's major town, Cruz Bay, is located on the southwestern side of the island, and in it is a restaurant I'll call "The Lobster Pot" (don't want any lawsuits!). This nice restaurant, hooked in the bend of a barely-two lane road that snakes down from the mountain, looks like your typical Caribbean dining establishment: wooden, painted with bright pinks, blues, and greens, mostly outdoor seating on either wooden benches or at plastic tables and chairs, ceiling fans lazily spinning overhead. I remember it being quite the popular establishment, and confirmed this on revisiting this tourist haunt just a few years ago.

At any rate, on this particular night, my family had finished up their meals and was enjoying their after-dinner fruity beverages. Now I'm not sure if you were ever a teenage boy or raised one of them; but from roughly the age of 10 – 23, we're human garbage cans. We'll finish all the food and (I'm annoyed looking back on it as a 31-year-old), easily burn off all the calories in the next couple of hours.

It just so happens that at this time in my life, I was in a rice pilaf phase. I know, what a lame phase. But I dug the whole salty thing, and eating thousands of tiny pieces of food (miss you, Mitch Hedberg). In this instance, my mother just happened to have left a sizeable portion of delicious-looking rice pilaf on her plate.

"Mom, can I have the rest of your rice pilaf?"

"Sure BenBo," and she slid her plate over, probably taking a sip of a piña colada as she made the transfer.

And me, the carefree teenager in paradise, gobbled it down. Every last grain of seasoned rice. That's when I started to get really thirsty. That's always my telltale sign that I've eaten something I'm allergic to: I involuntarily try to swallow something that's not there. I start drinking lots of water, trying to flush it down. The base of my molars start to tingle, like I just chewed a piece of tinfoil. The reason is that my throat is swelling closed with hives, so my throat thinks there's a piece of food back there that needs to go down. It needs to come out.

My mom noticed that I was beginning to turn a strange, bright red. "Ben?" she asked uncertainly.

By now I was out of water and sweating profusely. Things felt pretty awful.

As an animal, scallops are pretty cool. 'Scallop' is pretty much a comprehensive term for 'clam,' and it's fascinating to watch the little guys swim. It's a two-sided shell, and they kind of 'clap' backwards in the water, propelling them forward. I respect that, it looks neat.

If you happen to catch one of these suckers, or a dozen of them, common recipes recommend butter, olive oil, salt, pepper, and to pan sear them. When done, they look like little white discs of fish, and smell quite good.

And boy are they juicy.

That night at The Lobster Pot, Mom had scallops. As they sat on her plate, that tasty mix of butter, olive oil, and steam dripped from the scallops and oozed all over the plate. Rice is in the food kingdom of "sponge." In fact, thousands of tiny sponges. The pilaf had soaked it right up, so I had just consumed a pile of scallop juice.

Poison.

There are no hospitals on St. John. The Roy Lester Schneider Hospital on the nearest island, St. Thomas, is a 30-minute water taxi ride away followed by a cab ride along winding, two-lane roads. That's just too much time. So alternate plans were made.

As step one, my father ran to our rental jeep to fetch the bottle of Benedryl which, given the increasing frequency of allergy reactions I had been experiencing, the Cobers never travelled without. My mother then wasted no time measuring out the prescribed dosage, doubled it, and ordered me to guzzle it. For the uninitiated, Benedryl is a deep pink liquid, commonly cherry-flavored, that is insanely sticky but not very thick. It comes in alternative forms, like pills (seasonal allergies) or creams (insect stings or poison ivy), but the liquid is where it's at.

According to Benedryl's website, the substance staves off allergic reactions because of an ingredient called diphenhydramine hydrochloride, which is an antihistamine. In my experience, however, the liquid is made up of one part stale cherries, and four parts horse tranquilizer.

After taking the weirdest, non-alcoholic shot that restaurant had probably ever seen, we sprinted to our jeep and careened through the unlit, tropical back roads to our rental home. Reminds me of that scene in Jurassic Park where Wayne Knight is driving the JEEP through the tropical storm.

During the bumpy and slick ride, my mother and brother's fiancé sat on either side of me in the back seat, furiously scratching my chest and back. According to my grandmother, who also had a variety of allergies, this could stimulate blood flow around the lungs and hold off The Reaper as the hives swelled larger and larger around my airways. They honestly didn't know if it would work.

As we neared the house, I told them that I could feel my lungs relaxing, and it was getting easier to breathe. The combination of a nuclear bomb's worth of Benedryl and "The Scratchening" had kept me alive one more night. I asked my mother recently what she remembered about this night. Her response:

"It was an unbelievable situation. I have never been convinced that there wasn't a higher power watching over that situation; because given the seriousness of your allergy to shellfish, you should've died or at least gone into anaphylactic shock, there's just no question. I'll never forget that night." There are a lot of lessons. First, it is simply amazing how easily a tiny allergen mistake can happen. I was a hungry, growing boy; my mom had leftover rice pilaf; what's the harm?

Second, a solid combination of clinically-verified medication and good, old-fashioned knowledge gained through experience can go a long way.

Lastly, with the ever-looming threat of hidden food allergies, it astounds me how much freedom and independence my parents gave me as a child. I am eternally grateful, as I feel that parenting decision contributed a great deal to the person I am today, but it must have been terribly worrisome with a number of close scares like this one.

At the top of this chapter, I noted that these little allergen booby-traps are often hidden at the bottom of delicious, well-intentioned dishes. But not always... sometimes they're hidden inside things you shouldn't be eating in the first place. Such is the adventure of eating abroad!

"Doo-doo-doodle-do Doo-doo-doodle-do Doo-doo-doodle-do Doo-doo-doodle-do Doo-doo-doodle-do Doo-doo-doodle-do Doo-doo-doodle-do Doo-doo-doodle-do!!!!!!!" (In case you're not brushed up on your composers, that was John Williams' Olympic Fanfare).

In 2010, I travelled with my girlfriend (now wife) to Vancouver with a couple of friends for the Winter Olympics. It was an incredible week. The city of Vancouver is absolutely stunning, seated beautifully on English Bay with snow-capped mountains everywhere you look. The shadows of the towering skyscrapers were filled with amazing accents and delicious smells from around the world, all emanating from country-themed tents surrounding Olympic Park. We got to hold one of the torches, meet some Olympic volleyball players, pose for a photo with Al Roker, and enjoyed the best day of skiing I've ever had in my life: Whistler, with barely anyone else on the mountain.

I didn't attend any events - I was invited too late for there to be any tickets of any kind still available. However, we did watch the Canada vs. US hockey match in the basement of a Mexican restaurant. Canada won three to two in overtime, if you recall, and I've got to say I'm actually pretty fine with USA not winning. It was pretty amazing to be in the home of hockey after they won the gold in a sport so beloved, it could virtually run for Prime Minister.

Our lovely hosts, friends of my girlfriend's from Northwestern University, insisted that we needed to go out for Dim Sum. At the time, I had neither heard of, nor tried, Dim Sum, but two words convinced me that I needed to have it: Chinese Brunch.

Two things I find absolutely delicious: Chinese food and brunch food. Combining them sounded absolutely incredible; so on our last morning in Vancouver, we went out to this "authentic" dining experience. And it definitely was authentic. Fortunately, our host spoke Cantonese, and so she was able to translate and order a bevy of delicious dishes. We reminisced about the amazing week we had had while alluring smells simmered from the kitchen, and waiters and cooks shouted back and forth to us. At last, after what was torturously forever, trays and trays of sumptuous cuisine arrived at our table. Exotic odors poured out over the table: sweet and salty dishes, tangy and fruity, irresistible. I dug into the familiar: noodles, rice, buns, and meats, but finally the lid was lifted from a peculiar little pot, filled with little orange triangles. I licked my lips.

"Oooo, and what are these?" I inquired, spooning one of the morsels onto my plate.

"Chicken's feet," our host replied.

I'm sorry, what?

Another learning opportunity for me: chickens' feet is a very popular Chinese dish. The feet. Of chickens. The things that run around in the dirt and chicken poop in chicken coops. With claws. Chicken feet.

She assured me they were delicious and very well-cleaned. After some overly dramatic reactions, just for the sheer fun of it, her husband and I finally goaded each other into trying one. The thing is, the flavor wasn't that bad: a thick, tangy, orange-like sauce with a hint of spice. A little like the all-too-common General Tso's chicken. But the texture. The texture is what killed me. I could feel the little rivulets of the chicken's skin on my tongue. The only way you can eat these things is to bite a toe off the foot, then work it around in your mouth until you can pull a knuckle free, then spit the knuckle onto the plate and swallow the remaining "meat" and tendons. (That was officially the grossest sentence I've ever written). But I did it; I powered through it, and I ate myself a chicken foot; because gosh-darnit, I was travelling and trying new things.

But the bravado was short lived.

With two feet removed, we could now see deeper into the pot. And what that revealed, besides more knuckly chicken feet, were tons of boiled (maybe steamed) peanuts. Come. On! Really?! Why sneak them in anyway? I'm convinced, by how often unlisted peanuts are sneaked into dishes, that no one actually likes peanuts. But there's this massive overstock of the little %&*#ers, so restaurants have to sneak them into food where they serve NO beneficial addition, just to try and deplete their rotting reserves. So now everyone goes wide-eyed, and the laughter of the chicken feet quickly subsides, because they all know I'm allergic to nuts.

"I need to go to the hospital," was all I could mutter. We quickly paid the bill, and fortunately the nearest hospital was just a few blocks down the road. We hustled into the ER, everyone continuously asking me how I was doing, and thus I had my first brush with Canadian healthcare.

In the United States, you sign up with a private healthcare company (sometimes you get it through your employer), and pay a monthly fee (called a premium) to have healthcare through that private company. Then there's your deductible, which is much larger than your premium. You need to spend that amount of money on your own medical costs before the healthcare company will begin to cover a specific percentage of your medical costs, and that percentage varies wildly depending on what medical thing you need. Your monthly premium payments don't count towards reaching this deductible, and that deductible resets every year, even if you've paid all the way up to it.

In Canada, you pay a very large dollar amount in the form of a healthcare tax up front to the government every year; but from there on out, any single medical thing you need, from a doctor or hospital, is entirely free. Everything. Burn your hand on the stove and need treatment? Free. Terrible allergies and need to see the doctor? Free. Lose a leg in a car accident? Free. The kind of health expenses that annihilate families for generations in America do not exist in Canada. Coming from a family that has poured tens of thousands of dollars into my allergies over the decades, this blew my mind as the Canadians in the waiting room of the ER explained it to me. But I of course experienced the downside to free healthcare as well, the one often pointed out by its opponents. In the ER, we waited, and we waited, and we waited. We waited for nearly an hour, and were never seen. Now, to be fair, this wasn't my first rodeo with an ER, and I've waited for a long time in plenty of American ERs. But this was a bit worse in the Canadian ER, we were just never attended to.

Fortunately, and still without explanation, I never had an allergic reaction. In fact, the strangest part through it all was that I didn't feel anything. No hives, no sick stomach, no sweating or thirst. To this day I can't explain why the nuts didn't influence the chicken feet; but somehow, by some great fortune, they didn't. My girlfriend and her friends had watched me, tensely, for an hour, waiting to see me turn red and keel over on the waiting room floor. But it never happened; and without a reaction of any sort after an hour, we walked on out of there and headed home.

Man, would've been awful if my last meal on Earth was chicken feet.

# Chapter 6: When Allergies Hunt You Down

Some allergies are easier to hide from than others. If you're allergic to shellfish, stay out of the ocean (picture Chief Michael Brody running down the beach screaming "Get out of the water!" at the Annual Allergy-kid Beach Bash). If you're allergic to cats, you sadly have to convince yourself that your friend Karen, with that big furry American shorthair, might not have been that great of a friend after all. But it's a whole different story when your allergies (duhn duhn) can come out of the water (duhn duhn) … And hunt. You. Down. (Queue intense JAWS crescendo)

When I was just a young pup with itchy eyes and a runny nose, I loved bugs. Our house backed right up against the woods; and so with plastic terrarium in one hand and a net in the other, I'd run out into the woods in warm weather to track down fascinating, cute crawlies (get over your "creepy" crawly self, that Easy-Bake-Oven for boys has given bugs a grossly unfair stigma for more than two decades now!)

The word on my bug-love was out. My grandfather in Pennsylvania had a friend, Mr. Sellers, who owned an apple orchard. Every time we visited, my grandfather had a shoebox from Mr. Sellers filled with (dead) bugs found in his orchard – the best of which I remember was a massive, Chinese mantid. In the '90s, we still had clearly-delineated "boy" and "girl" things – and even though "bug catching" wasn't a girl thing, my mother likes to remind me that when we moved to Ohio in the summer of 1990, it took only a matter of weeks before a lot of the kids got "bug boxes," even the girls. We'd run around in mobs, into people's gardens, under decks, swooping up everything from butterflies to wolf spiders.

Heck, in high school, there was a senior year project where kids had to collect bugs, preserve and pin them, and present them to the class. I made a good coin every year from about second to fifth grade as high school students paid me up to a quarter per bug to do the dirty work for them. This entrepreneurial enterprise was further rewarded more than a decade later when I took entomology as my college science credit – but "running drunk at night through a field swinging a butterfly net" is a story for another book...

Back to the tale of venomous survival. One fine summer afternoon, I was dashing through the neighbors' yards, swinging my green net to and fro, snatching up bumblebees. Now, if you're unfamiliar with Apidae bombus, these are the fat and fuzzy bees you'll see lazily hovering between flowers, seemingly with no real rush or plan. Sometimes you'll see them crawl out from underground or from a hole in the wall, most likely where they've been aging their honey-hooch.

I had collected three of these flying pom poms in my net, and was returning back to my driveway where my terrarium was waiting, so that I could study them for a lengthier period of time (I didn't just catch bugs as a business, I was fascinated with them and studied every detail of their anatomy). I had my index finger and thumb wrapped around the netting, so as to trap the three buzzers, suddenly far more energetic and annoyed bees, from flying out the now-one-inch mouth of the net. And as I crossed the street, merrily skipping along, that's when one bee stood up for all bee kind. He wouldn't take the injustice, and he wasn't going to fight the Man with sit-ins or passive aggressive social media statuses. He stung. And that's the first time I was stung by a bee. And it was also the first time I was reminded that my allergist had said I was allergic to insect stings.

I howled and screamed and dropped the net, holding onto my throbbing thumb, and spinning and running across the street (I clearly remember spinning around, but in retrospect I have no idea how that was supposed to help). I ran into the house through the garage screaming "a bee stung me!" like the Earth had just opened up and an army of evil bee men were storming through the neighborhood. My mother thundered down the stairs in a frenzy and got me a pack of ice and told me to lie down on the couch.

She immediately called my allergist - whom I'm rather sure we had on speed dial – and she, receiving frequent calls from us, had a dedicated red phone for our family. The allergist said I needed to lie down and that my mother was to watch my stomach for any sign of hives. IF said hives showed themselves, we were to immediately rush to the ER. (I want you to picture the movie Gremlins; and I'm the sweet little Mogwai Gizmo, watching my belly in terror after water's just been spilled on it).

So we sat there together, my shirt pulled up to my chest, my eyes unblinking and me holding a numbing plastic bag of ice to my thumb, and my mother watching my belly for the slightest bubble of redness.

An hour went by. And then another. And another. And nothing happened.

My mother phoned the allergist, who was only partially relieved. "That's great news," she said. "So now he can never get stung again. Many kids who have allergies to insect stings don't have a reaction to the first sting. But the second sting... the second sting can be fatal."

So for the next 17 years, I avoided any flying, stinger-armed creature like it was carrying a nuclear warhead tipped with Ebola and the bubonic plague. I avoided beautiful gardens, fruit stands, open soda cans in the park, and squealed and ran from any bee or wasp like little Ms. Muffet. But as I stated before, bees hunt two things: pollen… and fear.

It was the summer after college, and I was working at a summer camp in northern Wisconsin as my "Capstone Class" (i.e. internship) to get my degree in tourism management. I was co-head counselor, shared a cabin with one other staffer, and it was the last summer with my beloved pickup truck – so I had it pretty good.

The catch was that it was an all-girls camp. That means that there were just three men on the entire property – myself, the head of the horseback riding camp (with whom I shared a bunk), and the head chef who lived in town. Now, many of you (those favoring the female persuasion) might be thinking this sounds like a sweet deal. But A, for the majority of the summer I was still dating my college sweetheart and I'm a dedicated man; and B) even if I was single, I can't think of a better way to stir up huge controversy and drama (read: get fired) than hitting on a counselor at an all girls' camp. So alas, I focused on doing a good job and learning as much as I could about running a summer camp (my then-dream job).

I had survived two thirds of the summer –a tornado literally passing right by camp, pre-dawn polar plunges in the lake, a management blow-up where someone thought I was gunning for their job, and my longest experience as a minority representative (merely one of two men living full-time on property, amongst 150+ women and girls). I could see the finish line: I was job-hunting for Fall, apartment searching in my hometown, and writing my final report for Professor Gower, when IT happened.

Head counselor honestly meant three things: help train the staff before camp starts, conduct staff reviews (which were generally defensive and awkward – try telling people how to do their job better when they've been coming to the camp since they were seven), and wear about 1,000 hats to fill in when and where it was needed. For me, this meant a summer of demolishing condemned cabins, running rainy-day activities, setting up the climbing wall, teaching sailing, cooking meals for 120, playing music, tracking down scary noises in the woods at night, and a million other things. What this also meant is that I was often on lifeguard duty.

So here I was lifeguarding at the lakefront one afternoon. This camp was very remote with a very small lake that bottomed out around 40' deep. The waterfront was a simple dock parallel to the shore, and then a roped off swim area maybe 70' across and 20' out into the lake. Any farther than that, and there were thick, long weeds growing up from the depths that felt like a thousand Jason Vorheeses clawing at your feet. Within the swim area, underwater visibility was zero, and the bottom was a gross, mucky silt. Needless to say, missing child drills for lifeguards were a nightmare.

I was sitting on top of the wooden lifeguard chair with a float draped across my lap, writing the letters of the alphabet over and over again with my eyes across the swim area. (This is a lifeguard trick to make sure you're covering every inch of a space, not repeating back and forth lines, and to keep you from getting bored. Few people know that lifeguarding is actually pretty boring – because, unlike Baywatch and FOX News like to suggest, rarely does anything interesting happen).

As an important side note, camp counselors often have camp names. These names are typically bestowed by fellow counselors during "pre-camp," the 1-2 weeks of training prior to the arrival of campers. You earn your camp name either out of honest kindness, where it's representative of a great part of your personality; or you earn it after doing something really stupid or embarrassing, kind of how you earn a fraternity pledge name. For example, at one summer camp, my camp name was "Bounce," because I taught the camp song "Little Bunny Foo Foo" and I could actually jump really high back then, despite being 5'4" in stature.

So this particular summer, I had earned the camp name "Mufasa," based around the notion that I was GENERALLY mature at camp; and as the oldest guy there, was a sort of father figure. But as any child raised on Disney can tell you, we know things don't turn out well for dad-lion.

So there I was – sitting on my wooden Pride Rock of sorts – watching over a group of about 20 kids around 12 years old splashing and playing. All of a sudden, I feel an incredibly sharp pain in my right shoulder, and whip my head over to find a wasp hovering angrily just a few inches from me. If he had had eyelids, they would've been squinting and had he had teeth, they would've been gritted. My first thought was that I had noticed a hole burrowed into the wood of the chair (on which I was leaning back against), and of course I should've known something stinging lived in there.

The second thought that went through my head was to scream out loud, at the top of my lungs, the F-word. That's right, the word. The big one. The Queen Mother of dirty words. The f-dash-dash-dash word.

The giggling and splashing stopped, and 20 heads turned in shocked horror as their "father figure" roared the F-Bomb from atop Pride Rock.

"Everyone out of the water!" I screamed as I leapt down the six feet from the chair onto the dock, tossing the float to the co-lifeguard, and began a mad 200-yard dash across the camp to my cabin. There in my bedside drawer was my EpiPen, which I knew could buy me some time before emergency medical help could arrive. It was a trade-off: running meant speeding up my oxygenation and blood flow, speeding up the wasp venom travelling through me. But if I didn't run, I might not make it to the EpiPen.

I made it to the cabin. I started throwing things out of the drawer as I searched for the needle, found it, and ran outside my cabin to administer it. In my rush for medicine, I hadn't had the chance to tell anyone what had happened or where I was headed. So, in my mind, I wanted to make it easy to find my body after I went unconscious from the wasp venom. Wearing swim trunks, it was easy to slam the needle into my outer thigh, and then I sat in the grass and tried to slow my breathing; and in effect, slow the progression of the evil wasp juice. Word had spread, and the camp director came running up to evaluate my status. Fortunately, knowing my allergies, she had called 911.

And there we sat together in the grass, me breathing heavily, her patiently trying to calm me, and us both waiting for my eyes to roll back into my head and pass out face down into the grass. And ten minutes passed. Then 20. Then 30.

It was a full 45 minutes before the ambulance finally reached the middle of the forest, where I was loaded into the back of it in the staff parking lot where the kids couldn't see. My state? Perfectly fine. Not a shortness of breath, not a scratchy throat. Not a single, friggin' hive. And then I rode to the hospital – an hour to the hospital – on the most uneventful, sheepish ambulance ride ever. Sort of a "so hey, you guys come out here to the forest often?" Got to the hospital, was under watch for a while, and absolutely no effect from the wasp sting at all. None whatsoever. Well, of course, no physical effect. Paying for the ambulance and the hospital visit annihilated any money I made that summer. Thanks US healthcare system. Should've been Canadian, eh?

That fall when I returned to Ohio, I went back to my childhood allergist and got another one of those delightful skin tests that even Hellraiser's Pinhead would go "ew, yeesh!" And sure enough, I was no longer allergic to insect stings. At SOME point in the previous 17 years, I had outgrown it. There was no way of knowing. And to think of all those afternoon strolls in botanical gardens I missed out on…
☐

# Chapter 7: Hormones are Allergic to Reason

Human beings have been making mistakes for more than 200,000 years. We tried to pet a "kitty," and were promptly eaten by a saber tooth tiger. We thought the peasants would tolerate our lavish tastes, and soon our castles were torn to the ground.

But no mistake is more commonly made than that in the pursuit of hormonal urges.

I started in college working towards a degree in acting, hoping to help people learn to cope with life's problems through witnessing performances in which people triumphed over them. When I learned that 1% of actors are actually working in theater at any given time, 1% of that 1% are in television and film, and that the people who can actually afford tickets to the theater might not be the ones who need it most, that dream quickly faded. Nevertheless, I gave it two years...
It was my freshman year of college, and I had been cast in a small student production called Blinded. The 40-minute short was about the dangers of mentally abusive relationships, rather than physical. And I, living the beautiful, glorious dream of the rollicking good times of the theater, got to play the leading role – the psychotically abusive boyfriend. Makin' Mom and Dad proud, one $15,000 tuition payment at a time. However, all was not lost in this dark and tragic affair. I was fortunate enough to be cast opposite the stunning Danielle, with a flourish of exotic Latin looks and just my height (a rare find indeed). And at the time of this show, I was single. Only months before had I parted ways with my high school girlfriend, the first time I was single in two years, and I was quickly plunged into the exciting, insane, dramatic world of freshman dating.

During our second week of rehearsals, late one night in the black box theater, it came time to rehearse our second date; which, to my sincere enthusiasm, culminated in some serious making out. I had been so excited to get to this point in rehearsals that I had greatly overlooked the fact that I had never been taught how to stage kiss. The most action I had ever gotten on stage was a peck on the cheek from the frontier schoolteacher in my 6th grade play Tumbleweeds. Beyond that, my knowledge was limited to what I had seen in the movies and on television.

So there we were, sitting in the dim light on a couch in the middle of the dark theater, Danielle's perfume wafting its way around my shoulders and making my head spin in the most delightful of ways. My last line was delivered, and the director leaned forward and said "now kiss." I paused, my heart racing, Danielle giving me a sheepish and alluring smile, and I turned to him and had to admit my ignorance. "Like, really kiss?" She giggled, he smiled, and responded, "you'll have to sell it." So I shrugged turned back to Danielle, who had an equally growing smile (I like to think we both might have been looking forward to this – it at least made it easier), and we began to kiss passionately.

It was good, really good. The director never said cut, so we just kept going. Freshman theater was a good choice, I began to think to myself. But then…then I began to notice something strange. Something…something tasted wrong. I pulled back and whispered, "you taste just like the smell of peanut butter." She smiled slyly and whispered in my ear, trying to actually sound sexy, "that's because I just ate a Reese's Peanut Butter Cup."

If I had thought my heart had been pounding before, now it was roaring to escape my chest. "What?!" I gasped. The director stood up, "What's wrong? Why are you stopping?" "Yeah, I had one while we were on break, why?" she asked innocently.

I jumped up, my mouth suddenly beginning to turn dry amongst the new coating of fatal peanut butter on my tongue and cheeks. "I have to go! I have to go right now!" And I bolted out of the theater, without explaining anything. Now, in retrospect, it's fun to reflect on what the two of them must have been thinking: a young freshman passionately making out with a fellow actress late at night, and suddenly leaping to my feet and running out of the room. But as I sprinted across campus, trying to make it to my dorm room before my throat closed, the thought didn't cross my mind.

I made the half-mile dash in time to bolt up three flights of stairs and blow my dorm room door open. I rummaged through my drawer, pulled out my EpiPen, and plunged it into my thigh as I felt my tongue begin to swell in my mouth. My throat was starting to itch as I jumped up and into the bathroom, and found a bottle of liquid Benadryl (the good stuff). I took two shots of that, threw the bottle on the floor, and plopped down on my bed, waiting to pass out. I texted my roommate, who just so happened to ALSO be the director of the show. Rehearsal was cancelled, obviously, as he came thundering back to our room.

I jumped up, and we stood at the ready to run out the door and to the hospital, but I grabbed his arm and said, "wait, hold on a second." We sat back down, and I just calmed my breathing, watching the walls and the floor, concentrating on slowing my heart rate. Then, minute by minute, my tongue began to shrink in my mouth and I could talk normally again. The hives began to subside in my throat, and my breathing became normal. And the redness in my face began to vanish. That night I learned two things:

1. Kissing someone who has recently eaten one of my food allergies results in a minor, temporary allergic reaction.
2. Danielle had the Kiss of Death my mother always warned me about with girls.

# Chapter 8: Stuffed Crap Cakes

Meeting the parents is a terrifying event for everyone. I don't care who you are, or how brave of a game you talk, it's an exciting and nerve-racking experience for everyone involved. For the parents, they're wondering what monster is ruining their little baby, and maybe picturing what their grandchildren are going to look, spawned from the mix with this outside genetic soup. There are a thousand judgments every second, hidden beneath a shimmering veneer of white teeth and "It's so nice to finally meet you."

For the son/daughter, everything's on the line. They obviously like this person, hence bringing him/her to meet the parents, so there's some vision of the future in mind. It's the culmination of, "Look Mom and Dad, who have raised me since I couldn't feed myself. I have taken everything you have taught me about love, intelligence, the world, life, goodness, respect, and legacy, and this is the person I have chosen to potentially carry on our family lineage! Have I done well?!" Yeah, THAT'S not terrifying.
As for the date, they're right in the same boat. They're trying to earn the respect and liking of the parents, because they like this boy or girl, and want to be in the parents' good graces so they can proceed down this road of love and partnership. The parents are gatekeepers; if things don't go well here, it's going to be a VERY bumpy road if you keep trying to go down it.

That's why he/she has asked the son/daughter tons of questions about their parents (memorizing key facts to demonstrate investment during the meeting), and probably agonized over tonight's outfit to demonstrate maturity and that 1) Goodwill is not the only store at which I shop and 2) I do laundry at least once per full moon.

Such was the situation in which I found myself in the fall of 2008 at a private dining club I'll call Macallan's. I was introducing my parents to my girlfriend, Jennifer, for the first time, and we were sharing a lovely early dinner overlooking downtown Cincinnati. Jennifer was very nervous about the meal, as she had never made it to the "meet the parents" stage with any previous boyfriends. I, as well, was nervous about the dinner…because Jennifer had never made it to the "meet the parents" stage with any previous boyfriends.

But, things were going quite well – there were stories being shared, laughter, engaging conversation, and no huge slip-ups like spilling wine all over the table or calling someone by the wrong name. In fact, one of our best laughs came from the terrible typo on this fine dining's menu: "Stuffed Crap Cakes." Now that's right over home plate of my mother's funny bone, and we enjoyed making up tales of the restaurant running out of crabs, and needing to come up with something quick on the spot for tonight's seating.

I laughed, but I should've taken it as a red flag…

Jennifer and I decided to share the Chicken Wonton as an appetizer. I'd never had chicken wontons before; but we both liked Chinese food, chicken seemed like a safe bet, and it wasn't something with a huge mess potential like soup or bruschetta. On the menu, in italics, the chicken wonton was described as something along the lines of:

*Tender, marinated chicken in a fried, flaky crust.*

No misspellings, and that sounds pretty straight forward and safe, right?

Wrong.

Two little fried triangles resembling Indian samosas arrived between us about 20 minutes later. They smelled delightful. We each politely took one, with linen napkins draped across our laps, and began to demonstrate to my parents that we weren't post-college, starved cave-people.

And they tasted fabulous – salty with a bit of sweetness, and still piping hot from the kitchen. The conversation continued as the sun began to set behind the restaurant, casting the skyscrapers of downtown Cincinnati in iridescent oranges and pinks.

And then I got thirsty. Really thirsty.

I started pounding my water as politely as possible, and then I noticed that Jennifer was doing the same. And then I felt it, the scratching at the back of my throat. I leaned over and whispered to her "Are you feeling all right?" And she shook her head.

"What is it?!" My mother jumped in nervously. My mother is a bit hysterical when it comes to any health or comfort-reducing incident (if you've read this far though, you can kind of understand why), but we were trying not to alert her...yet. We kept scanning the room for our waiter to ask what was in the chicken wontons, but that was the exact time he had chosen to catch a flight to Dubai, rent a car to drive into the desert, dig deep into a sand dune, put on some headphones, and disappear from the world into "Enter the Wu Tang." "I'm going to go ask the hostess," said Jennifer, as she politely excused herself from the table and we nervously looked at our empty water glasses. I was now starting to feel the heat around my face and the scratching in my throat was getting worse...this was going to be a bad one.

"What's wrong with her? Is everything ok?" asked my mother.

"Everything's fine, she's just not feeling well." I was doing my best at trying to keep the situation from escalating to full blown code red. I needed confirmation from Jennifer before sending everyone into a panic. "She's just using the restroom."

Five tense minutes ticked by, when Jennifer finally hurried back to the table, a bit breathless. "Escuse me Ben, a moment?" she gasped, as she pulled me from the table out of my parents' ear-shot. "The wontons are stuffed with peanut butter and fried in peanut oil," she whispered in pure fear. WHAT, MACALLAN'S?! HOW DO YOU NOT PUT THAT IN THE DESCRIPTION ON THE MENU!?

We stood there in shock, calculating and evaluating. One of the things that had brought Jennifer and me together was her list of strange allergies; and one of them, a shared allergy to peanuts. She looked terrified – it was her first serious allergic reaction.

My mind began to race. What to do – should I call 9-1-1? Have my parents drive us to the ER immediately? Or should I try to drive us to the hospital? In a matter of five seconds, here was my train of thought:

1. My parents will drive too conservatively and we'll never make it in time. We could be in serious trouble, and risk them getting in an accident by being too worried.
2. The last allergy ambulance I called (The Wisconsin Wasp) took 90 minutes roundtrip to come get me and take me to the hospital. We could be dead before it gets here.

3. When I've had allergic reactions before, it's taken roughly 20-30 minutes for the serious reaction to happen. The hospital is about 20 minutes away. I think I can get us to the hospital before I black out.

As calmly as possible, as to not alarm my parents, we returned to the table, where I said, "We're not feeling well, a little bit of a mild allergic reaction I think. We're just going to grab some Benadryl, and then we'll be right back." We then calmly walked out of their view, then slammed into the elevator and headed down. We were headed to the hospital, racing to get there before anaphylactic shock set in on the both of us. We hit the parking lot and my 5-speed Mazda 3 in a single bound, and were off. I started racing through the streets, slowly approaching red lights, checking both ways, and then running every single one. I called 9-1-1, hovering around 3rd gear to keep the speed going without having to shift.

"My girlfriend and I are Northbound on (I forget the street) and are both going into anaphylactic shock from an allergic reaction. Can we get a cop car to escort us immediately to the hospital or an ambulance to meet up with us?" I shouted, my heart pounding.

"I'm sorry sir," the operator responded, "but we can't give police escorts. You'll need to stop the car and wait for a cruiser or ambulance to arrive, and they can drive you to the hospital."

"How long will that take?" I asked desperately.

"I don't know sir, I'm not seeing any cars in your immediate area," she responded, something to that affect. I pleaded with her that we needed to safely get there as soon as possible, but she insisted we stop and wait.

"There's no time!" I shouted and hung up the phone. We pulled the car over in the dodgy northern Kentucky neighborhood, and there were two EpiPens in the glove box. I honestly wasn't sure what the epinephrine would do to me while driving – if it would make me erratic at the wheel and I couldn't finish the drive, or if it would boost my heart rate too much and cause an accident. I just didn't know, but I knew Jennifer was in even worse shape than I was, and I needed to prolong her just a bit more. "Get out of the car!" I shouted.

I grabbed an EpiPen, ran around the car, and knelt down at her leg. "I'm so sorry, but this is going to help. You're going to be ok," I told her. She had tears in her eyes and was so scared, but we hiked her dress up to mid-calf, and I plunged the syringe into the tissue and held it while the drug went into her system. I pulled it out with a drop of blood, and we jumped back into the car.

I continued to race down the streets, carefully running red lights, following my GPS to the nearest hospital. I did my best to comfort Jennifer as we drove, "Just hold on, you're going to be ok. Stay awake, keep talking to me. Tell me what you're feeling. You're going to be ok, just keep your eyes open." I sincerely felt like Christian Bale in Batman Begins, where Rachael has gotten a dose of Scarecrow's fear toxin, and he's racing back to the bat cave with her in the bat mobile, screaming "Rachael, hold on!!!" Except in my story, my car was a lot lamer and my throat was closing.

Fortunately, Jennifer seemed to be doing a bit better than I was, but she wasn't in the clear yet. She too felt hives swelling in her throat and her chest began to turn a bright red. This was the worst allergic reaction she had ever experienced, and I felt terrible for being the one to put her in that situation. Me, allergy man, bubble boy, who was supposed to have been on the watch for this kind of stuff all my life.

Incredibly, I turned a 30-minute drive into a 15-minute drive by running all the red lights – and not a SINGLE cop car in sight (WHAT?!). I flew into the hospital parking lot, and couldn't find a single parking spot near the ER door or any crystal clear directional signage as to where to park. Thankfully, I spotted an EMT tidying up things at the back of an ambulance. We pulled up and I rolled down my window. "Help!" I shouted. "We're both going into anaphylactic shock right now. Where can I leave the car?"

The ridiculousness of the situation hit him, and he responded, "Right there, just park in the fire lane!" So I whipped the car around and parked about 40 feet away on the hill where he had directed me. We hopped out of the car, and began to make for the sliding doors. Thumping against my thigh in my pocket was the second EpiPen. At the time, EpiPens ran about $75 a pop, but I didn't even want to guess what a hospital would charge for epinephrine. So my plan all along was to use it after I arrived at the hospital, but before admitting myself to the ER.

There on the hill I began to unbuckle my belt to drop my dress pants and slam in the needle. However, at that very moment, walking up the hill about 20 feet away, was a large Amish family. How do I know they were Amish? Beards, vests, straw hats, dresses, and bonnets. Now, I'm not a god-fearing man; but, if there was a moment that would test the heavens and send a bolt of lightning through the top of my head, it would be the moment I drop my pants in front of a group of Amish children.

So I buckled up my belt and we dashed for the ER. The doors opened and we ran through the metal detector (yep, the best hospital in Cincinnati is in that kind of neighborhood). It began to buzz wildly, and the cop behind the counter began to shout. Jennifer, with tears in her eyes, screamed back "We're both going into anaphylactic shock!" He let us go. "Check us in," I said, as I saw the sign for the restroom, and I made for it. Once inside, the pants dropped and the needle slammed in, dropping it in the garbage can. I'm sure I broke some kind of law or hospital policy, but I also might've saved myself $1,000.

I was in and out in about two minutes; and by the time I got back into the lobby, Jennifer was gone. A nurse was waiting for me; and after informing me that Jennifer was already being treated, she rushed me back into a hospital room. It was a large, circular space with curtained rooms around the edges, and counters, machines, and cabinets in the middle. I was de-clothed and put into a hospital robe, and placed into the bed. An IV was slipped into my arm and an oxygen mask was strapped around my face. As my world began to go hazy and my eyes grew heavy, I remember my ER doctor came in. And to this day, I'm not hesitant to say it at all: she was the most badass health professional I've ever seen.

She looked like a fighter jet pilot who had just ejected out of her F-16. I had never seen anything like it. She was in a dark green jumpsuit with zippers and pockets all over it, her hair pulled back into a tight bun. She was direct, no bed-side manners, and there to make sure I didn't die. It was awesome. "Is Jennifer ok?" I whispered.

"She's going to be fine. Now we're going to take care of you," she said, and my world went black.

As I'm told, a couple hours passed, and I opened my eyes to find my parents sitting in the room with me. I could hear my own heart monitor beeping steadily next to me. (When I tell this story in person, my mother likes to jump in here to say that when she arrived at the hospital, my heart monitor was so erratic and fast that she earnestly thought she had arrived to watch me die.) I felt exhausted and hazy, but my throat was no longer swollen – but my voice was tired. I managed a smile, and my parents came to my bed-side.

"Is Jennifer ok?" I asked.

My dad smiled, "Yes, she's fine. Her parents got here about 30 minutes ago." I'd like to point out that this is how our parents met: with both of us on life support in the ER. So next time someone tells you that they had a terrible date and that meathead on Tinder didn't work out, tell them at least their parents didn't meet for the first time while they were both hospitalized because of friggin' chicken wontons.

Jennifer used to also like to point out, during this point in the story, that my mother came to check on her after checking on me at the ER. Jennifer was conscious, and had fared far better than I had in the end, but was also nude beneath her hospital gown (as one commonly is). So, on the first date meeting my parents, my mom saw her standing, from the back, in her hospital gown. So that's just grand...

At any rate, after about 20 minutes, the curtain to my room slid open and a large police officer stepped in. "Are you Ben Cober?" he asked me. My father spoke up, "I'm Rod Cober, I'm Ben's father."

Immediately what went through my mind was the 20+ red lights I had ran through to make it to the hospital. I had no idea cops would track you down INSIDE the ER, even after nearly dying, to arrest you. If I hadn't already embarrassed my parents enough, I was about to absolutely shame them.
"I need the keys to his vehicle," stated the officer matter-of-factly. "He failed to put the parking brake on, so the car has rolled down the hill into an ambulance and we need to move it." That's right folks, WHILE UNCONSCIOUS in a hospital bed, I HIT an ambulance.

None of us batted an eye. "They're in my jacket pocket," I said. Dad got the keys, handed them to the officer, and he walked out. No tickets were written, no cuffs were closed, no damages were filed. Somehow the cop and the hospital had mercy on me.

Jennifer went home with her parents, and by 11 p.m. I was discharged and driven home. I could tell, deep, deep down inside my mother, there were a thousand "I told you sos" wanting to be muttered about being careful when eating out, but I think she was just glad I had lived.

Jennifer and I stuck it out for another year and a half after the Wonton Incident. But like Sandra Bullock says to Keanu Reeves at the end of 1994's Speed, "I've heard relationships based on intense experiences never work."

☐

# Chapter 9: Love Doesn't Hurt, It Kills

This could have been my final story, because it's about the time I thought I was going to die.

It was the fall of 2005, and I had just transferred to the University of Illinois in Champaign-Urbana. I had met the most wonderful woman, Melissa, in Sailing Club, and everything was clicking 100%. Things had gone so well that we had at last reached the aforementioned step – meeting the parents.

This story finds us on a sleepy, rainy Saturday morning in the suburbs of Chicago, IL. We had driven up for the weekend so that I could spend a Saturday riding around the sprawling metropolis meeting not just her parents, but virtually every member of the family. There are few times in my life that I can admit this, but I was sincerely nervous. I really, really liked Melissa, and I wanted to make a great impression. The interesting twist here was that half of her family is Polish and half her family is Filipino – both coming from their respective countries about fifty years ago. Now I absolutely love learning about and experiencing new cultures, but I was entirely unfamiliar with Polish and Filipino culture. There were about 1,000 mistakes that could've been made, especially with such a large family with tiers of importance. I come from a very small family, about 20 names to remember, and I was walking into a massive, extended meet-and-greet.

So to prepare, Melissa took me to her favorite Chinese (Red flag! Red flag!) restaurant in her home neighborhood for lunch. The plan was to recap all the family members and dynamics, so I was ready and prepared to meet everyone later that afternoon. I was one of the top students in my class – I was great at memorizing and taking notes – so I was totally ready for "Melissa's Family 101."

We sat across from one another in a comfortable booth with classic Formica tables, and began to review the family tree as the rain pitter-pattered against the window behind us. We got a couple tall classes of water, I think I ordered my go-to General Tso's Chicken, and the restaurant brought us complimentary spring rolls. They were the biggest spring rolls I had ever seen, almost like taquitos, and I began to dive into mine hungrily while Melissa explained who had how many cousins, who was older than whom, and where everyone lived. It was the most delicious spring roll I had ever eaten — so juicy, so fresh, still steaming hot. I had barely looked at it as I gobbled it down while listening to Professor Melissa. I finally came up for a breath of fresh air, and went to set down my two-thirds eaten spring roll on the plate. Before I could completely let go of it, a small, pink circle rolled out and spun around on the little plate, finally wobbling and landing still in the middle.

"Is that a shrimp?" I asked. I didn't know shrimp could get so small: the thing couldn't have been bigger than a nickel. Maybe it was a vegetable I wasn't recognizing.

"That's definitely a shrimp," said Melissa, her eyes growing wide. She looked up at me as the color began to drain from her face. I inspected what was left of my "spring roll" to find that it was packed to the brim with the little pink circles. I had just consumed four inches of shrimp. My heart began to race.

"Oh my god, what do we do?!" said Melissa, beginning to panic.

"Calm down, calm down," I said. "Maybe I've grown out of it. My allergist said that I might grow out of some of my allergies, and it's been a while since I've been tested. Honestly, if I were still allergic, I should be dead by now."

That did not comfort my date at all. We carried on our family preparation talk; our dishes arrived, and we ate our lunch, Melissa carefully watching me with every bite.

And then the throat got scratchy. I began to drink gulps of water. "Maybe I'll just flush it out," I said. But the more water I drank, the worse I felt. I was trying to be strong, hoping it would go away. But it didn't.

"We need to leave, I need to get some Benadryl," I said. Melissa's face filled with worry. We quickly paid the bill, our half-eaten lunches still warm on the table, and jogged through the rain and hopped into my pickup truck. Just down the block was a Walgreens, and we casually parked the car and walked in. We bustled down to the allergy and flu aisle, found the liquid Benadryl (knowing that this is generally the all-purpose nuclear bomb for allergic reactions), and I did a complete first: I consumed something inside a store before paying for it. We ripped open the box, cracked open the bottle, and I drank 2/3 of a bottle of Benadryl. We waited a second as I breathed heavily from the gulping, and then a sharp pain shot through my gut. I don't know if it was from the shrimp fighting back against the onslaught, or the coma-inducing level of Benadryl I had just pounded, but my gut hurt like nothing I had ever felt.

"It's not working," I said. "We need to get to a hospital." Melissa ran to the counter to pay for the Benadryl while I ran outside to start the truck. TomTom was all the rage in GPSs at that time, so I punched in the nearest hospital. As Melissa hopped into the truck and noticed our destination, she said, "I've never heard of that one before – all I know of is Good Samaritan, which is about 20 minutes away."

Of course, being stubborn and a bit adrenaline-rushed, I said, "This one's closer," not even considering that Melissa had GROWN UP IN THIS NEIGHBORHOOD, and obviously knew it better than Mr. TomTom. So I put the truck in gear, and headed towards the hospital. The challenge was that I hadn't taught Melissa to drive a stick shift (we hadn't gotten to that fun date yet), so I needed to drive the truck to make it to the ER. I hadn't yet experienced the previous chapter's WonTon incident, so I didn't know how long a food allergy reaction took; and I hadn't yet experienced the Wisconsin Wasp, so I didn't know how long an ambulance could take to arrive. But TomTom said we were just 10 minutes away, and I felt I could drive that.

So we cruised along the (thankfully) uncongested, windy, small town roads as the rain gently fell on the windshield. And that's when things turned bad. The hives began to spread all over, and my body began to get very warm. Hives began to swell in my throat, and my breathing got more and more difficult. My eyes began to swell, and my field of view shrank as our ETA dwindled from five minutes, to four minutes, to three and down. The new reaction though emerged in the form of hives over the back of my head. I began fiercely itching behind my ears, and could feel huge welts beginning to grow. It was a painful experience, and I was thankful that I heard TomTom belt out "You have reached your destination."

My two front tires hiccupped over the curb into an empty parking lot, and we came to a stop beneath a large, red sign reading:

"Planned Parenthood."

Apparently TomTom's definition of "hospital" is a little general. Not only was Planned Parenthood completely useless for my current state, but it's also exactly where I'd love for Melissa's devoutly Catholic family to learn the destination of our first Chicago date: Planned Parenthood. Awesome. And they weren't even open – to provide any kind of assistance.

We were out of time. My eyes had swollen to the point that I could barely see anymore; and despite 10 minutes of observation, Melissa still hadn't learned how to drive stick. So I turned to her and gasped, "Call 9-1-1." And she did. And thus began the longest 10 minutes of my life.

We sat there in silence as the rain beat down on the windshield of the truck. Every symptom I mentioned earlier greatly increased to the point of me considering if my death bed would actually be a death seat. Hives expanded in my ears to the point where it sounded like listening to voices under water. My eyes had all but swollen shut, letting in just a little bit of light. My body ached all over, with my insides twisting and turning – from head to toe I felt like I was being pushed through a meat-grinder. The itching on my scalp had gotten so bad that I started to draw blood. And the worst part of it all was that my throat had swollen so much that it felt like I was breathing through a coffee straw after sprinting a 5k. All the while, Melissa sat there, helpless, watching my body die. We had checked the glove compartment – there was no EpiPen. All we could do was wait.

And at last, sirens blaring, the ambulance roared into the parking lot, and paramedics pulled me from the truck. I could make out Melissa describing to an EMT what had happened as I was lifted into the ambulance and the doors were shut behind me. I didn't notice the needle sliding into my arm, but I received an IV.

Then someone's face came into view over mine, a fuzzy blur, and said, "All right, your girlfriend told us that you took a lot of Benadryl, which is a downer. And we just gave you adrenaline, which is an upper, so the next fifteen minutes could be a little crazy!"

And then, just as I was passing out from the downer, I overheard the driver casually talking with Melissa in the front seat of the ambulance. "So, you're from around here?" he asked. "Ah, that's cool. Where are you going to school? Do you come back home often?" Obviously he was trying to make small talk to distract Melissa from the intense situation in the back of the ambulance, but all I could think was "I'm not dead yet man, don't hit on my girlfriend!"

The EMT who warned me about the narcotic concoction in my bloodstream hadn't been kidding. One second I'd be in a deep, deep unconscious dream, and the next I would be wide awake, my heart thundering against my rib cage with the power of adrenaline. And then, without warning, I'd slip back into a deep sleep. And that's where I stayed for the rest of the day.

As Melissa tells it, we quickly reached the hospital and were immediately admitted to the ER. I lay there, unconscious, with IV in, monitors attached, and oxygen mask strapped on. And that's when Melissa had to fish out my cell phone to call my parents.

"Hello? Mrs. Cober? Hi, yes, this is Melissa, your son's girlfriend. Um, Ben's fine, but we're at the hospital…" is exactly how the conversation went down. And there my mom sat, 320 miles away, unable to do a single thing. After years of trying to protect me from stupidly putting fatal stuff in my mouth, it had finally happened on a grand scale. In all honesty, I'm glad I was unconscious – that's not a conversation I would've liked to overhear. So once again, if you ever come home after a terribly dull or frustrating date, just think to yourself, "At least I didn't have to call his mom to tell her that I literally almost killed him."

I woke up that night in Melissa's mother's guest room after phases of consciousness. I had been discharged, recovered and all better. I have to admit, it was a pretty dramatic move to dodge meeting the family that weekend, but it definitely bought me some more time to study up on the family tree… The epilogue to this story is that the following spring, the Qdoba on campus had a "Best Worst First Date Story" competition for Sweetest Day (an even more manufactured couples' holiday than Hallmark's Valentine's Day). I felt I had this one pretty much in the bag, so I wrote up an abbreviated version of what you just read and submitted it to my favorite fast food joint. Within a week I got a reply email from Qdoba saying, "We've ended the competition. You win." Our story was posted at the cash register for a month, and we won a huge, free nacho bar for as many people as we wanted to invite. There in the party room above Qdoba, we retold this story to our Sailing Club friends who had helped bring us together.

The epilogue to the epilogue is that nine years later, Melissa and I were married on the shores of Lake Michigan. Having just celebrated our first anniversary, we've dodged any further allergic catastrophes, and we know we'll be rolling the dice soon to see what allergies our poor children end up with. At least we'll be ready…

# Chapter 10: The Message

Last fall I celebrated my 31st birthday by having a mystery dinner in a pitch black room (don't worry, we asked ahead of time what would be served) and enjoyed a delicious chocolate cake Melissa made from one of the four "Baking without Eggs" cookbooks that sit in our kitchen.

I could not have dreamed up a more patient, understanding wife regarding the ridiculousness that is my seasonal and food allergies. She understands when we have to call room service in a hotel room to bring us non-feather pillows; she doesn't grumble when we can't visit a friend's house for more than 20 minutes because they have cats; and she gets that I have a weird fear of baseball stadiums because everything's covered in peanut dust. But that doesn't mean that she doesn't get what she needs. Many a time when we're out to dinner, she'll spy an irresistible shrimp dish, oyster platter, and boy does she have a weak spot for shellfish sushi! She'll say "Babe, I'm sorry, but I'm getting shellfish tonight." We'll have one final smooch before dinner, and then she dives in. And when I go out of town for work, she simply goes crazy, and it's 48 hours of quiche, peanut butter and jelly sandwiches, and crab and shrimp.

[Fascinating side note: when I broke up with my high school girlfriend, after she graduated two years ahead of me (knuckle-bump), she got a job waitressing at Joe's Crabshack because she knew I would never step foot in there].

I'm far more careful today with my allergies than I've been in the past. I'm familiar with situations that are going to get me into trouble, and eating out can be neurotic experience. No matter the restaurant, I start by flipping through and skipping over anything that contains any of my food allergies. Then, with what's left, I consider what I'm in the mood for (chicken, beef, veggie, pasta, pork, etc.). And from that, I narrow down by price. Consider that pattern every time you eat out, and what options you'd have. On TOP of that, consider that you've got to make sure to ask about how utensils/grills are cleaned in between dishes (so, despite my wife's love for sushi, it's kind of nuts for me to go to a sushi bar when every other thing a knife touches is shrimp). Despite this carefulness, I simply can't avoid close calls. It's a part of life, and one of my key takeaways for you, the allergy haver, the allergy parent, or the allergy friend: the world will not change for you.

Recently in Chicago I almost died. I love Indian food, and there's this delicious sweet rice pudding named Kheer that you eat after your meal. It's just perfect. SOME places mix nuts in, and not like whole nuts, as you might imagine in a pasta salad, where you can see everything in it. No, some places grind them into a super fine powder that makes it indistinguishable from the pudding. But then OTHERS don't mix in nuts at all. Wherever you go though, the ingredients are just listed "sweet rice." So I plopped down a little cup of it at our table with a bunch of friends enjoying a nice Sunday morning Indian brunch, and went to wash my hands.
In my absence, Anna figured out that there were probably cashews in the Kheer. She, Aakarsh, and my wife all looked at each other in a moment of terror, to which my wife responded, "How long has Ben been in the bathroom?" They started to get up in panic and head for the restroom, when I popped out and cheerfully strolled towards the table. "Are you ok!?" Anna asked nervously.

"Of course," I responded. "Why?"

"Um, don't eat that," said Aakarsh. "I asked and it has nuts in it, LOTS of nuts. Why did you get that?!" Great question...

In an earlier life, I worked at a museum that celebrated Bugfest every June. With my aforementioned interest in bugs, I was actually excited to enjoy one of the most alluring activities that Bugfest had to offer: eating bugs. You could try chocolate covered scorpions, spicy crickets, and mealworms baked into brownies. The shipment of crickets had just arrived, and I rushed over to the natural history museum offices to try one out. Just before I popped the spicy little bugger into my mouth, Amanda said, "Hold on a second, look at this on the box." And on the little Tic-Tac sized box were the tiny words "Do not eat if allergic to shellfish." A few minutes of Google later, we learned that the main protein in the exoskeletons of insects, chitin, is the same protein found in the shells of crustaceans; hence, no bug munching. Man, if reincarnation is real, I better not come back as a bird!

A friend recently took a big adult life step of buying a house, and naturally he had a lovely housewarming party for all of his friends. With the varied interests and cultural backgrounds of the attendees, the potluck dishes were colorful, aromatic, and mouth-watering. One guest plopped down a huge pot of a dish that looked similar to biryani (a favorite of mine, but I have to ask for 'no nuts'). She rattled off the fantastic ingredients of rice, veggies, and spices, and everything sounded fantastic. I took a few heaps onto my plate, sat comfortably down at the dining room table next to some new friends, and took a big scoop onto my fork. Just as it got close to my face, I noticed the familiar, pale, curved little shape hiding amongst the rice. "I'm so sorry, excuse me, what's this little guy here in the rice?" I asked. "Oh, that's a cashew," she pleasantly responded. That seemed to have been omitted from her earlier list of ingredients… another close call.

But it's not all bad; sometimes there are perks to having allergies! When I was 13, my father strapped the lawn mower to my hands and told me to go mow the front lawn. I had seen him and neighbors do it countless times, and it actually looked like a lot of fun! 45 minutes later I walked back into the house with my eyes completely swollen shut from the stirred up grass pollen. I have never mowed a lawn since.

Early on in my life as a food allergy kid, I was intensely picky, and a large portion of that was due to a fear of accidentally eating something my allergist and parents said would kill me. In general, I avoided foods where not all the ingredients were visible – think no sauces or complex mixes of things (intricate salads or... well... biryani). I was eight before I tried my first hamburger, 10 before I was ready to switch up my standard ham and American cheese on white bread for lunch, and 12 before I had my first Coke. Ethnic dishes of any kind simply never found their way to my plate – it was pretty much plain chicken, pork, veggies, and simple pastas for many, many years.

But that's no way to live! There's a whole world out there of incredible spices, storied cooking styles, strange roots, fruits, and veggies, and tantalizing meats! And I love to travel internationally; so what am I going to do, ask for a ham sandwich? No! We must dine upon the local cuisines! So I've taken the responsibility to become familiar with the ingredients and preparation steps of food I'm interested in, and popular dishes in countries I visit. This, delightfully, has led to safe eating of a wide array of delicious dishes from Thailand, India, Ethiopia, Japan, the Philippines, Greece, Peru, Israel, Italy, and many more. In addition, I've come to try and be far more adventurous with dishes that I know do not fall within "eggs, nuts, or shellfish," which has led to some pretty strange eats. Chicken feet, tripe (cow intestine), fish eggs, alligator, water chestnuts (I'm not proud of how long it took me to figure out that they're not actually nuts), salmon eyes and cheeks, and even cuy (Peruvian guinea pig). Despite my food allergies, the world can still be a big, delicious buffet.

But here's the catch: while a keen eye will keep you safe with food allergies, there's no way of avoiding seasonal allergies. Through spring and fall, when the pollen, mold, and ragweed are at their greatest strength, you will be at the mercy of Mother Nature. I've never not had an allergist, and they've always armed me with weapons to fight her off:

- Daily allergy pills like Claritin, Claritin D, Zyrtec, or Allegra
- Ventolin and albuterol inhalers
- Weekly allergy shots (or less often when building up a tolerance)
- Local honey in my tea
- Air purifiers
- Frequent showers to wash off mother nature
- The nuclear bomb of allergy fighting: Benedryl

I'd even add construction goggles, gloves, and a facemask to that list; because a couple years ago when a best friend was getting married and wanted to pick flowers the day before her wedding for her bouquets, I couldn't refuse a friend's wedding request. So, I got heavy duty goggles, thick gloves, and an industrial gas mask, and I hit that flower patch. My allergists would've been horrified.

But no two allergists are created equal, and I've never found two that agreed on everything. In St. Louis, my allergist was insistent that I needed to get allergy shots every three weeks. And it was awful! Not the shot itself, but there would be immense swelling in my triceps for 24 hours, and they would actually radiate heat.

The first time I came back home from college, I had terrible allergic fits; hence, every Thanksgiving and Christmas family photograph for the last 12 years has me with a red nose and watery eyes (not because I was dressed up as emotional Santa). It didn't take long for us to realize that I had lost my allergy tolerance to the dander of the two Jack Russell Terriers I had grown up with. Just so you understand, that meant that when I was home for the holidays, there was no playing with the dogs, laying on the carpet, or sitting on any furniture on which the dogs had sat. Ho… ho… ho.

So, when my wife and I decided to get a dog, we got a "hypo-allergenic" dog, an Airedale Terrier puppy. And I've never had any problems with him…

However, when I got my new allergist after moving to the Pacific Northwest, he had a lot to disagree with. First, he explained that allergy shots don't work after puberty, so I should no longer take those. Second, he said that "hypo-allergenic" was just a marketing term developed in the '90s to sell different breeds of dogs, and the test comprised just taking a Q-tip along the floors where the dogs had been and measuring the dander density. In essence, he said it was bogus and was better to not even own a dog. And lastly, he said since there's such different flora in the PNW compared to the Midwest, that fall allergies virtually don't exist. Yeah, tell that to the sick days I've taken, the thousands of tissues I've gone through, and the recently-replaced air filter on our home purifier.

Since my allergies weren't getting any better, I switched allergists – not more than a couple miles down the road – and my new allergist said that allergist was straight up wrong about everything he said. I'm on a monthly allergy shot regimen now, after going weekly for a few months, and my seasonal allergies are the best they've been in a decade.

So what can you do?! Allergists don't agree and give conflicting information, and some days are just downright debilitating with the sneezing, coughing, and running nose. This leads to my final four lessons of living a totally fulfilling, and potentially awesome, life with allergies.

## 1. You Are a Sneezing Snowflake

While you may have similar allergies to others ("hey, cool, we both get itchy around grass!"), your allergies are wholly unique and are your own. You will have different severity of allergies, different laundry lists of allergies, and may discover them (or they will develop) at different points in your life. You may be told that you're allergic to all nuts; and even when your blood work comes back from the Mayo Clinic saying there are three types of nuts you actually should have no reaction to, your allergist may still tell you to avoid all nuts.

What I'm saying is: there will come a time in your life when you realize that you know more about your individual allergies than anyone else, more than your allergist, more than your doctor, more than your parents, and more than your spouse.

Only you have lived your collective life of experiences, mistakes, advice, and allergic encounters. You know better than anyone else what sets you off, what makes you feel better, how long it takes for reactions to kick in or wear off, and what it's like to live with the daily annoyance (and threat) of allergies.

And, I hate to say this, but it's not going to get better. In my 26 years of awareness of my allergies (because come on, who remembers much before the age of five), I've seen some incredible advances in our world: we cloned a sheep! We put a Land Rover on Mars! We discovered the Higgs Boson particle! We're making artificial limbs that not only have dexterity, but can feel! We're developing equipment that can help the blind see and the deaf hear! We mapped the human genome, can target-treat cancer cells, and we've got the HPV vaccine! You know what science has done for shellfish allergies in 30 years? We've gone from "Don't eat shellfish" to "Um, well, uh, try not to eat shellfish." For seasonal allergies, we've gone from "take pills" to "take pills." There is no cure, and it doesn't seem like many scientists are taking finding a cure very seriously at all. So you've got this for life, kid.

So, you must become your own expert. Research, read, consult, discuss, but take it all with a grain of salt. You will need to find what works for you, as an individual, because you are a beautiful, sneezing snowflake.

## 2.  Drop Your Entitlement

You have allergies. Your nose gets runny when flowers get frisky and you might die if you eat a peanut. That is your responsibility, and no one else's. Let me say that again: that is your responsibility, and no one else's. People who love you may help keep watch over you, so that you're not an idiot and eat biryani laced with nut dust. But not a single person in the world, besides you, is responsible for your allergies. YOU have to be mature. YOU have to be vigilant. YOU need to take ownership of your actions and choices, and never, ever, be confrontational, rude, or demand accommodations for your allergies. You do not have cancer, you do not have lupus, you do not have heart disease. This is a manageable life situation and you should not expect empathy or pity. As travel journalist Rick Steves always says, "travel graciously." That means you, or if you're a parent, and that the following should be avoided:

a.  Demanding restaurants display or write out all the ingredients on their menus
b.  Demanding your child's non-profit summer camp build an extra dining facility so your child can safely eat in another room where nuts have never been (I've seen this)
c.  Demand airlines, or your airplane seat neighbor, neither eat nor consume nuts (you should drive or take a train next time – it's not an entire industry's obligation to bend for you)
d.  Demand your child's teacher vigilantly watch out for their food allergies (they've got hundreds of other children to manage and remember)
e.  Demand a friend hosting a party, or their wedding, have foods that are safe for you to eat (pack a meal)

f.  Or virtually anything else where you demand someone or some organization alter their operations to suit your individual needs.

Now notice that I always used the word "demand." That's sort of what entitlement is: expecting people to do things for you because of your situation. That's simply rude, ego-centric, and not realistic for living in this world. However, there are far politer ways (i.e. "travel graciously") to ask for these things, but don't get upset if the answer is "no." You may ask your server for a list of ingredients; you may ask the summer camp if special accommodations can be made for your child at meal time; and you may ask your neighbor not to explode a bag of peanuts next to you. And they have every right in the world to say "no," and you have every right in the world to take your business elsewhere… but not to be a jerk about it.

Part of this is that few people, except fellow allergy sufferers, will take your allergies seriously. I don't think I've actually ever had a serious conversation about allergies, outside of medical professionals, and my parents, about it. Most people find it pretty funny, or don't think it's that serious. For example, here's a transcript from a recent Louis C.K. bit, that actually had me crying laughing.

"You know you have your bad thoughts, hopefully you do good things. Everybody has a competition in their brain of good thoughts and bad thoughts; hopefully the good thoughts win. For me I always have both: I have the thing I believe, the good thing, that's the thing I believe. And then there's this thing [scowl], and I don't believe it, but it is there. It's become a category in my brain that I call "Of Course... but Maybe." I'll give you an example. Like, of course, of course, children who have nut allergies need to be protected. Of course! We have to segregate their food from nuts, have their medication available at all times, and anybody who manufactures or serves food needs to be aware of deadly nut allergies. Of course... but maybe, maybe if touching a nut kills you, you're supposed to die. [raucous laughter] Of course not, of course not, of course not, Jesus. I have a nephew who has that; I'd be devastated if something happened to him. But maybe, maybe if we all just [cover our eyes] for one year, we're done with nut allergies forever."

And that's funny, I'm not going to lie. Be serious, internally, about your allergies. Be vigilant, be responsible, and remember the things that keep you healthy and alive. But don't take yourself too seriously, and don't expect other people to change their perception.

### 3. You and I... We Are Not the Same

You may think that, with my severe allergies to food and various environmental factors, that I would be more empathetic towards other people with dietary restrictions. And, in fact, you would be absolutely correct. I have great empathy for other people I meet or know who are forced to adjust their standard of living because of a naturally-occurring affliction like diabetes, irritable bowel syndrome, or lactose intolerance. I feel I have a bit of a shared bond with these people, as we were born, or developed, biological issues that require us to be cautious about what we eat so as to not cause serious internal problems.

However, my food allergies have hardened me against empathy with people who get to make choices about their diet. Over the years, I have heard too many times things along the lines of, "Oh, you're allergic to shellfish? Yeah, I hear you, I don't eat hot dogs because I think their contents are gross;" or "Oh, an allergy to eggs, yeah, I know that's tough. I swore off eating chicken because I don't want to support the awful environments in which chickens are raised;" or "Yeah, nut allergies, I heard about that on the news. Actually, in the same broadcast, they talked about how orchard workers are often underpaid immigrants working really long hours, and I support both the minimum wage and immigrants not taking low-paying jobs away from Americans, so I stopped drinking orange juice."

You and I, friend, are not the same. You have the luxury, yes, the luxury, of making choices about what you consume. You were born with no biological repulsion to this world. You look at a menu and your choices are "everything." So, without really taking a huge hit on your options, you have the luxury of making political and moral choices about what you eat, like going vegan, or vegetarian, or gluten-free, or anti-GMO, or to call French Fries 'Freedom Fries' (and then proudly revert back fourteen years later when you put a red, blue, and white filter on your Facebook profile pic). These are decisions, they're choices, not a burden you have to bear. Not something you have to seek treatment for or that can kill you with a little slip up.

Many of my associates make these choices; and they're cool about it. It's their decision, they're not an evangelist about it, and they live their life without expectation from others (as I try to do with my allergies). It's a (relatively) free country, and you have the opportunity to make statements about the world, and support industries you wish to, by making decisions and choices about what you consume. But too many folks I have encountered talk as though they deserve a badge for their choice, a place of honor, entitled respect.

But you and I are not the same, friend. I was born into a restricted world of food, you merely adopted it.

## 4. Live Your Life

And finally we reach the last, and most important, message of this book. Do not seek shelter. Do not hide from daylight. Ships were made for sailing, not for safe anchor at harbor. There is an immense, beautiful, exciting, fun, fascinating world out there, full of incredible, wonderful, kind, generous, funny, deep, and honorable people for you to meet. And I'm not talking about the 7/11 down the street: I'm talking India, Korea, Australia, Taiwan, South Africa, Argentina, Spain, Canada, Britain, and 157 other countries, each different from the next. Your instinct, if you're a parent of a child with allergies, will be to cover, coddle, protect, and shield your child from the world so that they don't die from accidental ingestion. But in my life experience, this is the wrong approach.

You, as a parent, probably hope that your child grows up to be an intelligent, free-thinking, confident, self-reliant, gracious, empathetic contributor to society. To help encourage that, you'll need to be brave and take risks with them, help them learn and master their own allergies, and help them gain the confidence that they can take care of themselves. Because when they turn 18 and head off to college (or elsewhere into life), and all you've done is shield them and been their vigilant guard regarding their allergies, they may end up at a Waffle House drunk at 2 a.m. and order an omelet thinking that French is a hilarious language and not even think twice that it's mostly made of their egg allergy.

Be brave, so they can be brave. Even with seasonal allergies: spring and fall, in most places, are absolutely beautiful seasons. Even if you have bad allergies, you can't sit inside on the couch for six months out of the year binge watching Friends with a box of tissues. You're going to miss the colors, you're going to miss the memories, you're going to miss life.

Yes, this book is filled with my near-death experiences. But this book is only a hair over 22,000 words. I could write billions of words describing the wonderful experiences I've had around the world with friends and family not fearing my allergies, dining in bizarre and crazy places, and strolling beautiful scenery packed with bright flowers, swaying grass, and big, broad, leafy trees. You must not fear the world, my friend, you must not hide from it. You must embrace it, explore it, learn from your mistakes, and try something even crazier next time.

My wife and I are about a year or two away from starting our own family. Some allergists say that allergies skip a generation (my grandmother Ida May (Ida May's Kitchen) had allergies, my mother and much older brother don't), but I'm prepared for anything with our kids. I hope that a lifetime of mistakes, lessons, and adventure has prepared me to be a great father to a little one with allergies (or without). I hope I can take my own advice, and not helicopter over them, protecting them from the world. I hope that I can teach them about their allergies, help them master them, and to not fear food, nature, and the world beyond our home. Because it's a sniffly, itchy, scratchy, coughy world out there, and no one should miss it.

# Epilogue: EpiPens and The Sequel

At the time of the publishing of this work, the great Mylan EpiPen controversy has been breaking news. As I've explained what an integral role EpiPen has played in my survival throughout these chapters, I'd be remiss not to comment on the issue and offer some final advice — about living with allergies and potentially living without the security and life-extending capability of EpiPens.

In the summer of 2016, EpiPen maker Mylan Pharmaceuticals doubled the 2014 price of its two-pack of EpiPens to $608, up 550% since 2007. EpiPen is the company's only big-selling, branded product, making up 12% of the company's revenue and 23% of its operating income.

During the same period of this 2007-2016 price increase, Mylan's CEO, Heather Bresch, gave herself a 671% raise, from $2.4 million up to nearly $19 million. Over the last five years, Mylan had the second highest executive compensation among all U.S. drug and biotech firms, with the top five managers totaling $300 million in salaries.

Now, EpiPens have been around for more than 25 years; and while the effectiveness of the drug hasn't improved, the demand has risen due to the aforementioned rising prevalence of food allergies. It's been noted that, during anaphylactic shock, you should use the second EpiPen after 15 minutes if emergency help hasn't arrived. EpiPens are not reusable, and they are voided if exposed to high heat, strong cold, or submerged in water. You need them wherever you might have an allergic reaction – so at all times you need a set in your car, at home, and at your office or school. And they expire after a year. That means, at a minimum, you need to buy three sets – at the time of this writing, $1,824 – every year, and more if you park your car in the sun or get rained on with one in your pocket. Strong health insurance plans will knock about $100 off each set, but those with no insurance or high deductibles get no reduction in the cost.

I should also mention that Mylan has a virtual monopoly on the consumer-delivered epinephrine market in the United States.

Now when Mylan made this announcement, Cincinnati lawyer Carl Lewis filed a class action lawsuit against Mylan with over 1,000 plaintiffs; New York Attorney General Eric Schniederman launched an anti-trust investigation against the company; and a US Senate subcommittee issued a press release in September 2016 stating that they would be investigating the price hike. Remember Turing Pharmaceuticals CEO Martin Shkreli, the "Pharma Bro," who price-hiked the AIDS drug Deraprim by 5,400% - from $13.50 to $750 per pill - in the fall of 2015? The guy who was later arrested that December by the FBI for securities fraud while at MSMB Capital Management? When asked about Mylan's EpiPen price-hike, that guy told NBC News that, "These guys are vultures" and asked, "What drives this company's moral compass?"

As a reaction, thus far, Mylan is offering an "identical" generic form of an EpiPen two-pack for about $300. In every other case, they have publically defended their price increase.
- *(Sources: MarketWatch, NBC News, Forbes, ABC News, Fox Business, and FOX News)*

So what's my point?

I suppose one could find some capitalistic irony in all this. I have told a number of stories in this book where an EpiPen bought me enough extra time to receive life-saving medical care. In that sense, it was integral in keeping me alive. So, how much am I willing to pay for a drug that has the potential to save my life? My parents might have said, "We'll find a way to pay for it whatever the cost!" (And that's exactly what it sounds like the executives at Mylan are counting on). On the other hand, if a family can't afford to have the drug on hand, then it's life-extending, or even life-saving, capability is, well, worth nothing at all.

If we even more-carefully managed our finances, we could probably afford the newly-priced EpiPens (I almost said "new EpiPens;" but remember, nothing's changed about the drug). However, that's probably not the case with most allergy sufferers in America. It's a really steep price hike, with no innovation in the drug or explanation that the ability to produce it is getting harder: so far, all signs point to, "So they can pay their C-Suite more money." As I've said before, EpiPens don't save lives: they may buy you some extra time during anaphylactic shock until professional, emergency help can be administered. These Pens expire annually, are very delicate to temperature and moisture changes; and if all goes well, you may never need to use one. But that doesn't mean that you won't be shelling out thousands of dollars every year "just in case." It is of my personal opinion that, as an allergy sufferer or allergy parent, that you should be outraged and fighting Mylan (and that's the drug company, not the beautiful and fashionable city if Milan in northern Italy).

So now you might be facing the tough, and arguably morally challenging, decision of whether or not to keep buying EpiPens; and if you don't, how to stay alive. Here are five tips to remember if you go the way of no EpiPens:

1. Remember that EpiPens are only good for things that'll send you into anaphylactic shock. If you don't have allergies that can cause anaphylaxis, you don't need EpiPens;
2. Learn your anaphylaxis-causing allergies well, and very carefully avoid them on menus;
3. Keep Benadryl on hand – it can really help in serious allergy situations;
4. Do not eat things just to be polite without knowing all the ingredients;

5. Have a general knowledge of the distance to the nearest hospital if you're going to be entering environments where a food-allergy reaction is a potential risk; if it's too far, consider not going.

# The Sequel!

If this recounting gains enough interest, I intend to pursue a sequel in which I share other people's stories of allergy survival and living great lives. If you would like to participate, please email your <4,000-word story to deathbylobster@gmail.com.

Stories will be told anonymously, and will be proofed for spelling, grammar, punctuation, and vulgarity (come on, think of the children) before publishing. I know there are plenty more people in the world, living full lives without stopping because of allergies: let's share those triumphs!

17673909R10057

Made in the USA
Middletown, DE
28 November 2018